What's the Use of Economics?

What's the Use of Economics?

TEACHING THE DISMAL SCIENCE
AFTER THE CRISIS

Edited by
Diane Coyle

LONDON PUBLISHING PARTNERSHIP

Published by the London Publishing Partnership
www.londonpublishingpartnership.co.uk

Published in association with Enlightenment Economics
www.enlightenmenteconomics.com

ISBN 978-1-907994-04-3 (pbk.)

A catalogue record for this book is available from the British Library

This book has been composed in Lucida using T$_{\!E}$X
Copyedited and typeset by T&T Productions Ltd, London

Contents

CONTENTS

Introduction: The State of Economics and the Education of Economists

By Diane Coyle

The financial crisis that started in 2007 and still continues is one of the origins of this book. The economics profession was not giving loud and effective warnings of an impending crisis in the months ahead of traumatic events like the bank run on Northern Rock and the collapse of Lehman Brothers. Even though many economists had been sceptical about the euro before it was launched, and many warned of bubbles in the housing and stock markets, the profession is evidently unable to propose any solution to the continuing crisis that can command a consensus. Different schools of thought about how to manage the economy battle for attention in political circles and in the headlines (see Wren-Lewis 2012). It is not surprising that events have led many economists, as well as many people outside the profession, to question the failure of economics either to send an adequate early warning ahead of the crisis or to resolve it quickly.

However, there was already a debate among economists about whether the mainstream of their subject was unduly narrow, continuing now as a debate about the extent to which the character of mainstream economics itself bears responsibility for the present crisis. Most economists— whether in the academic, business, finance or policy worlds—reject the wholesale criticisms made by non-economists and 'heterodox' economists, but nevertheless do question what aspects of the conventional approach to modelling might have contributed to the profession's pre-crisis blinkers.[1] And while exciting research was under way in behavioural economics, in institutional and development economics and in the well-being agenda, it was not clear that this had gained much traction in the core curriculum. The gap between the interesting questions or real-world problems and the workhorse economics being taught to students at all levels has become a chasm since the start of the crisis. There is in fact

---

[1]One prominent example was Krugman (2006), although it prompted some sharp responses from other economists, such as Cochrane (2009). (See also Coyle (2012a).)

a paradox: economics, particularly macroeconomics, is in a state of turmoil because of the crisis in the economy; but research in many areas of applied economics is in an extraordinarily fruitful period of scientific discovery thanks to new data sources and methodological innovations.[2]

Neither the failures of macroeconomics nor the successes of applied microeconomics are yet features of the undergraduate curriculum. It is only a slight exaggeration to say that students are taught as if nothing had changed in the past five years. This fact has crystallized growing employer discontent with the knowledge and skills of the new recruits they hire. As one employer said to me: 'Of course there has to be a lot of on-the-job training and experience of work. We are not so naive as to expect new graduates to be oven-ready. But we don't really expect to get them this farm-fresh either.' Following a series of conversations between employers of economics graduates in the United Kingdom—including the Government Economic Service (GES) and the Bank of England, investment banks and consultancies—a conference hosted by the GES and the Bank in February 2012 brought employers and academics together to discuss the state of economics and the state of economics education. The conference was the springboard for the essays in this book.

There are three themes that emerged from the conference discussions: the narrow range of knowledge and skills demonstrated by economics graduates; the questions raised by the crisis about the content of the economics they are taught, concerning both macroeconomics in particular and economic methodology more generally; and the barriers to curriculum and teaching reform in universities.

What Do Employers of Economists Want?

Taking the first of these, employers uniformly said that they find new economics graduates to be too narrow in their approach to the applied work they will be doing in their job, whether this is in the public sector, in business or in finance. Employers are aware of the risk of having unrealistic expectations of new graduates, and there are of course some especially able graduates, but on the whole they find that their new employees need more significant on-the-job training and experience than they would expect. The missing ingredients listed here are

- greater awareness of history or real-world context,
- practical knowledge of data handling,

---

[2]For more on this see Coyle (2012b). My earlier book, *The Soulful Science* (Coyle 2007), largely predates the crisis but discusses advances in the subject since the 1980s.

- the ability to communicate technical results to non-economists,
- understanding of the limitations of modelling or of economic methodology,
- a more pluralistic approach to teaching the subject, and
- a combination of inductive and deductive reasoning.

The first part of the book, 'What Do Employers of Economists Want?', looks at these gaps.

Dave Ramsden, as head of the Government Economic Service (GES) and Chief Economic Adviser to HM Treasury, makes the fundamental point that while life does not observe disciplinary boundaries, too many economists lack interdisciplinary knowledge or even interest. What is more, in policy-related economics jobs, the economist always needs to be aware of the democratic, political context:

> GES practitioners are engaged in how to produce useful guidance for decision makers from the incomplete information available today, within a multitude of constraints and overlapping considerations, to address an uncertain tomorrow.

He argues that students need to be taught a deep understanding of fundamental concepts, including cost–benefit analysis, develop broad quantitative skills and be given some grounding in economic history and the history of economics.

David Colander continues the same theme by looking at the economics undergraduate curriculum, which he argues should be broader than it is now while not covering every possibility. There is no single ideal curriculum, he suggests, given that the question is: how can we best teach economics with the economists we have and the skills those economists possess? What we should teach needs to reflect both what we can most effectively teach and what students can learn on their own, not what we would teach in some hypothetical world. What we teach does not necessarily reflect all of what we believe students should know.

Given this starting note of realism, Paul Anand and Jonathan Leape draw from a survey of GES members to discuss what these economists say that their jobs consist of and what skills they need. The chapter makes what should be an obvious point: that few people who get economics undergraduate degrees will become academics, yet many undergraduate courses teach a curriculum best suited to delivering future PhDs regardless. What professional economists typically do is apply their economics training in a variety of contexts and communicate the results to diverse audiences. The survey results show that this 'creative and synthetic' work requires a range of skills, including a knowledge of institutions, communication skills, an understanding of alternative empirical approaches and, above all, an ability to synthesize different types of evidence from diverse sources.

Stephen King highlights the same skills from his perspective in investment banking, some knowledge of and interest in the global economic context and the institutions of financial markets. He writes:

> I lament the fact that economists coming into the financial world struggle to relate what they have learnt at university to economic developments in the real world. I have asked recent university leavers how much time they had spent in lectures and seminars on the financial crisis. Most admitted that the subject had not even been raised. This is profoundly disappointing.

Bridget Rosewell adds that the gap between theory and practice extends to microeconomic analysis of the kind performed by many economic consultancies as well. Importantly, the lacuna in practical knowledge extends to data, with many graduates believing that to understand the concept is to understand the statistics: they have no appreciation of the way statistics are gathered or of the possibilities for collecting and using other data. What is more, many graduates also fail to appreciate that dynamics and feedbacks can lead to radically different propositions about policy and economic management.

Finally, in this section, Steven Schifferes focuses on the communication skills mentioned by every employer of economists. As he points out, communicating complicated ideas is a difficult challenge, given that there is little public understanding of economics to start with, and little public engagement by academic economists in the United Kingdom (or indeed in many countries apart from the United States). Yet the financial crisis has, among other things, highlighted both the public interest and the need for the profession to engage more effectively with the wider public. Retreat into the ivory tower is not an option.

Some of the responsibility for this has to fall on employers themselves. They typically expect the graduates they hire to have had relevant work experience or internships, which certainly help to prepare young people for the demands of employment. Students spend a great deal of time and energy finding these placements; employers could discuss with universities how to make them easier to arrange. More engagement in general between employers of economists and economics departments would surely be fruitful, helping the flow of information in both directions.

Economic Methodology and Teaching Economics

The second theme is that the crisis has served to underline some serious questions about economic methodology. These can be divided into general issues concerning the use and status of models and the range of techniques or approaches that universities should be teaching economics students; and specific issues about macroeconomics. Part 2 of the book covers the former.

Andrew Lo warns against 'theory envy'. As he says:

> We economists wish to explain 99% of all observable phenomena using three simple laws, like the physicists do, but we have to settle, instead, for ninety-nine laws that explain only 3%, which is terribly frustrating!

But the real lesson from physics is not that simple laws explain the universe, but rather that empirical verification of any theoretical prediction is what matters. Mathematical techniques gain meaning from solving actual empirical problems, and should be taught in that context.

John Kay argues that the academic economics taught to students has turned into the intellectual analogue of a computer game: an artificial and wholly deductive world. Students need to be taught inductive and empirical methods as well. This does not mean more of the statistical analysis of large data sets taught in university econometrics courses, but rather thinking about what evidence is needed to answer a specific question, and working out how to assemble it and collect data.

In his chapter, Alan Kirman sets the abstraction of modern economics from the world of practical business and policy matters in its historical context, highlighting the peculiarity that it has *not* been considered 'unscientific' to make assumptions about preferences or behaviour, yet assumptions about institutions or interactions between individuals have been so labelled. He argues that a completely different approach to modeling is required, using tools such as network theory, or econophysics, as well as the experimental methods and behavioural approaches already adopted by a growing number of economists. Kirman, too, emphasizes practical data skills.

Ed Glaeser points out the tension between turning out well-rounded young economists with a broad understanding of history or the global economy, and teaching the specialisms that will enable a thorough understanding of an area of applied economics. While arguing that the core of the discipline is not 'broken', he advocates more experience for students in government departments or consultancies as the best way for them to learn about the skills they might eventually need in their careers, as experience cannot be short-circuited.

Paul Seabright highlights the prior numeracy skills and critical thinking students have, or have not, learned at school. When it comes to the undergraduate curriculum, he suggests that:

> The most powerful improvement in economics education might be to find a way of teaching the subject that does not present it as an ever-more-successful approach to the truth about how economies work, but rather an investigation into a phenomenon that evolves as fast as we can keep up with it.

A course structured around specific economic problems, setting out the best current theory and evidence but also the tale of how economics got to that point and what puzzles remain, might be the best way to do this. Harold James advocates reintroducing economic history to the curriculum in some form because history teaches three important insights: the existence of patterns, the importance of uncertainty, and the prevalence of multiple possible outcomes. There is a danger of being over-simplistic, he adds, but 'the best way of thinking about history is as a way of testing conventional hypotheses—particularly when those hypotheses are being used to create market opportunities'.

MACROECONOMICS AFTER THE CRISIS

Turning specifically to macroeconomics, this is the area in which contributors' opinions diverge, rather than converging—a parallel, one might say, to the character of the current macroeconomic debate. Although all accept that the crisis has rightly prompted a re-evaluation of macroeconomics courses, some contributors suggest what could be described as evolutionary reform of the current curriculum.

Wendy Carlin sets out a way of integrating the lessons of economic history, the intellectual history of macroeconomic thinking, and the current workhorse macroeconomic model. This structure reflects the reality that macroeconomic theory has continually evolved in response to events: Keynesian aggregate demand management being a reaction to the Great Depression, the stagflation of the 1970s generating monetarism and the new classical synthesis. Now that the 'Great Moderation' has ended in the crisis, the policy prescriptions of the 1990s and 2000s—especially the strict separation of monetary and fiscal policy—are in their turn being replaced.

Jagjit Chadha accepts that the standard macro model has been proven to be too simplistic, but in addition to increasing its sophistication (with the introduction of banking sectors, for example), he argues that it should be supplemented with other well-known macro models that had fallen into disuse before the crisis but can do much to explain its causes and consequences. In particular, the global payments imbalances and Eurozone tensions are easy to explain in a conventional international macro framework using well-known models. Like Carlin, he advocates the integration of the ideas of earlier generations of macroeconomists into the framework of macro models with microeconomic foundations, contributing to a richer and more informative yet still rigorous model structure.

Roger Farmer agrees that mainstream macro has not been a waste of time, and that the formalism of models and the rational expectations revolution has been important and useful. In fact, he argues that the insights of New Keynesian economics need formalizing more thoroughly, as none of them includes the possibility of unemployment in equilibrium. The formal approach needs to be taught alongside economic history, history of thought and the use of data to ensure that students are sufficiently pluralist. Benjamin Friedman, on the other hand, describes pre-crisis macro as 'wrong-headed'. It has ignored the financial sector, whose expansion has been one of the defining features of the modern economy, and placed too much weight on the empirically incorrect assumption of rational expectations. It has forgotten that it is not money but credit that affects real economic outcomes, and that the institutional structure of financial intermediation matters too. Finally, macroeconomics has entirely ignored frictions and the impact of distribution. Macroeconomists need to research and teach the 'features of the economy in which we live, as opposed to some simpler alternative that we can readily imagine and easily model'.

Andrew Haldane also identifies some of these failings in his chapter, particularly the absolute failure of the orthodoxy to take note of the explosion in commercial bank balance sheets. The past few years have retaught an old lesson: that credit cycles are as permanent a feature as business cycles. But understanding the role of credit in the modern economy, with its complex interconnections in the financial system, requires the use of network models, he argues:

> Conventional models, based on the representative agent and with expectations mimicking fundamentals, have no hope of capturing these system dynamics. They are fundamentally ill suited to capturing today's networked world.

Paul Ormerod and Dirk Helbing go further still. They suggest it is 'back to the drawing board' for macroeconomics. Conventional dynamic stochastic general equilibrium models have no place in the curriculum, in their view, having proved entirely useless for policymakers. Echoing Haldane, they argue that

> We live now in a densely networked, strongly coupled and largely inter-dependent world, which behaves completely differently from a system of independently optimizing decision makers.

The representative agent approach must be replaced, and its replacement should set the research agenda in macroeconomics, according to Helbing and Ormerod. This is clearly far from the view of those contributors who consider that the existing macro framework being taught to undergraduates needs adjustment rather than replacement, and there will no doubt be a good deal more discussion among academics about what ought to constitute the core of macroeconomics teaching.

REFORMING UNDERGRADUATE TEACHING IN UK UNIVERSITIES

This wide range of opinions about macro indicates that the undergraduate macroeconomics curriculum is unlikely to change radically in the near future, as the content of courses is bound to lag behind the professional consensus. Nevertheless, the contributions emphasize the extent of the agreement that undergraduate courses in economics must change, and also the existence of some agreement on the specifics of the changes needed. The final section of the book turns to the third theme: the pedagogical challenge and the question of the incentives that academics face to either introduce change in their courses and teaching practice, or resist it.

This book looks at the UK context specifically, but similar issues apply to other countries, including the United States. Michael McMahon notes that students are dissatisfied about their contact with their lecturers, whose incentives in the UK university system direct their efforts towards research and publishing in a relatively narrow range of mainstream (mainly American) journals. He suggests that there are some simple changes that universities could make to save lecturers time, and some non-time-intensive changes that lecturers could make to their teaching techniques to bring their courses alive for students. He also points out that students themselves must appreciate that to benefit from university they need to read widely, think and discuss, and not just expect their lecturers to spoon feed them all they need to know to pass the exams.

John Sloman also discusses reform within the framework of the current set of institutional incentives, proposing mechanisms for sharing existing teaching innovations and best practice more widely. He notes the 'pressure on lecturers to get good pass rates—a pressure that is increased by various quality assurance procedures, encourages making assessments predictable and "teaching to the exam"'. Greater numbers of students, with strong expectations of success given the increased fees, are increasing this pressure. But he points out that there is a wide range of pedagogical innovations that universities and lecturers could adopt at reasonably low cost in time and money.

Jonathan Leape describes one particular innovation at the London School of Economics: the LSE100 course. Now (2012) in its third year, LSE100 is compulsory for all undergraduates, not just those studying economics. The course uses current issues of public debate to explore different disciplinary perspectives. An example would be looking at the financial crisis from the perspectives of economics, history and international relations, or at whether culture matters from the perspectives of anthropology and economic history. The aim is to broaden students' intellectual training by introducing them to the range of methodologies available for studying social science problems, as well as to issues of causality and—of particular relevance to economics students—to the role of inductive approaches alongside the deductive reasoning that prevails in economics.

Finally, Alison Wride concludes the discussion with a fundamentally important point. There has been a substantial increase in the number of economics students at university, and unprecedented interest in the subject thanks to the crisis. She writes that 'we will lose all credibility if we come out of the crisis without learning from it and changing what we do'. Students, entirely rationally given the fees they pay, expect to be employable, but they are being taught courses based narrowly on technical models, giving them skills that employers say are inadequate, as we saw in the earlier part of this book. Wride concludes:

> I do know that we have sent out graduates, many of whom have gone on to important roles in industry and the country, who have consistently undervalued risk and have not seen 'right and wrong' as anything to do with economics.

This must change. Economics cannot possibly emerge from the crisis unreformed. What we teach the next generation of economists is absolutely the right place to start our re-evaluation of the subject. The degree of interest in economics now presents an opportunity to enthuse students about its strengths and insights, and to demonstrate how absolutely relevant the subject is to 'real-world' events. The discussion that started at the conference that inspired this book has continued, with a working group consisting of employers and academics looking at skill needs, student requirements, specific barriers to curriculum reform, and other aspects of the institutional framework that hinder change. Past attempts to reform the teaching of economics have foundered on the existence of system-wide obstacles and inertia, so a coordinated effort will be needed. One early action will be a student conference to ensure that students are able to contribute to the development of the economics curriculum, and of the subject itself, in the light of the lessons we have all learned during the past few years. We can hope and expect that the enthusiasm of the students themselves will be an important source of momentum.

References

Cochrane, J. 2009. How did Krugman get it so wrong? Available at http://faculty
.chicagobooth.edu/john.cochrane/research/papers/krugman_response.htm
(accessed 5 May 2012).

Coyle, D. 2007. *The Soulful Science: What Economists Really Do and Why It Matters.* Princeton University Press.

Coyle, D. 2012a. The public responsibilities of the economist. Tanner Lectures. Available at http://www.bnc.ox.ac.uk/downloads/news/tanner_lecture_2012
_text.pdf.

Coyle, D. 2012b. Do economic crises reflect crises in economics? Rethinking Economics Conference Keynote Address, Stiftverband für die Deutsche Wissenschaft/Handelsblatt, Frankfurt am Main (23 January 2012). Available at www.stifterverband.de/oekonomie/coyle.pdf (accessed 5 May 2012).

Krugman, P. 2006. How did economists get it so wrong? *New York Times Magazine*, 6 September 2006.

Wren-Lewis, S. 2012. The return of schools of thought. Blog post available at http://mainlymacro.blogspot.co.uk/2012/01/return-of-schools-of-thought-macro.html (accessed 24 April 2012).

Contributors

Paul Anand
Professor of Economics, Decision Sciences & Philosophy, Open University

Wendy Carlin
Professor of Economics, University College London

Jagjit S. Chadha
Professor of Economics, Chair in Banking and Finance, University of Kent

David Colander
C. A. Johnson Distinguished Professor of Economics, Middlebury College

Diane Coyle
Director, Enlightenment Economics

Roger E. A. Farmer
Distinguished Professor and Chair of the Economics Department, UCLA

Benjamin M. Friedman
William Joseph Maier Professor of Political Economy, Harvard University

Edward Glaeser
Fred and Eleanor Glimp Professor of Economics, Harvard University

Andrew Haldane
Executive Director, Financial Stability, Bank of England

Dirk Helbing
Professor of Sociology, ETH Zurich

Harold James
Professor of History and International Affairs, Princeton University

John Kay
Visiting Professor, London School of Economics

Stephen King
Group Chief Economist, HSBC

Alan Kirman
Professor Emeritus of Economics, Aix-Marseille Université

Jonathan Leape
Director of LSE100 and Senior Lecturer in Economics, London School of
Economics

Andrew W. Lo
Charles E. and Susan T. Harris Professor, MIT Sloan School of Management

Michael McMahon
Assistant Professor of Economics, University of Warwick

Paul Ormerod
Partner, Volterra Partners; Department of Anthropology, University of Durham

Dave Ramsden
Head of Government Economic Service; Chief Economic Adviser, HM Treasury

Bridget Rosewell
Partner, Volterra Partners

Steve Schifferes
Marjorie Deane Professor of Financial Journalism, City University London

Paul Seabright
Professor of Economics, Toulouse School of Economics

John Sloman
Director, Economics Network

Alison Wride
Head of the College of Business, Economics and Law/Pennaeth y Coleg Busnes,
Economeg a'r Gyfraith, Swansea University

What's the Use of Economics?

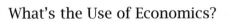

PART 1

WHAT DO EMPLOYERS OF ECONOMISTS WANT?

Making Economics and Economists Better: The Government Economic Service Perspective

By Dave Ramsden

In the conclusion of his valuable paper 'The macroeconomist as scientist and engineer', Greg Mankiw repeats one of the many famous quotations from Keynes's *Essays in Persuasion*:

> If economists could manage to get themselves thought of as humble, competent people on a level with dentists, that would be splendid.

For Mankiw:

> Engineers are, first and foremost, problem-solvers. By contrast, the goal of scientists is to understand how the world works.... For those interested in macroeconomics as both science and engineering, we can take the recent emergence of a new synthesis as a hopeful sign that more progress can be made on both fronts. As we look ahead, humble and competent remain ideals toward which macroeconomists can aspire.

Mankiw wrote this in 2006, a year before the first sign of the crisis emerged. The rest is history. Since then the failings of both economists and economics have been exposed.

Government Economic Service (GES) economists are professional practitioners of economics—very much at the engineering end of Greg Mankiw's spectrum. Here I will try and do two things: first, give a personal perspective, and second, draw out some practical next steps.

THE CONFERENCE

As an economic policymaker I take my share of responsibility for past errors. I feel more positive now about the future because of initiatives such as this one, debating the future of economics education. Above all, the debate has brought home the point that the biggest challenge is the behaviour of economists rather than the behaviours they seek to model and explain, whether at the micro or macro level. It is a real public good to have this debate because the ideas, energy and enthusiasm it generates will take forward the developments that we need to see in the use and teaching of economics, and in the discipline itself.

My first reflection concerns what we have learnt about the state of economics. Most professional practitioners like me have to rely quite heavily on the academic economic profession's opinion of what is best in modern economics. There have been broader advances: in understanding financial economics, behavioural economics and complex agent networks, for example. But it is worrying that, like the shock of the economic crisis itself, these do strongly suggest that the previous balance of emphasis among the scientists in our profession might not have been an entirely healthy one. The profession may have stifled the development and influence of other, also useful, approaches.

In the GES we quickly learn on the job that although rigour is important, so too is the need to join up the rigour from different disciplines. The real world does not respect any demarcations of disciplines, and policymaking is therefore intrinsically socioeconomic—and in government it is also always located within a wider democratic setting. Addressing the real world as a practical practitioner requires an interdisciplinary approach, and so for government there is a lot in Hayek's observation that if one is 'only' an economist then one is probably a pretty poor economist.[1]

For professional practitioners, it is not useful to define rigour as sticking to the formal stipulations of any particular school of economists. We do not tend to spend much time pondering over the heavily contested debates of scientific methodology anyway. But we *are* very interested in 'what works', and so we are increasingly concerned in microeconomics with rigorous evaluation, such as is laid out in HM Treasury's *Magenta Book*, which now accompanies the Treasury's *Green Book*. Unfortunately for evaluation in macroeconomics, there is inevitably a dearth of counterfactuals, and randomized control trials are not applicable. This is one reason, among many, that economic policy advice is not simply a matter of science; GES practitioners are engaged in how to produce useful guidance for decision makers from the incomplete information available today, within a multitude of constraints and overlapping considerations, to address an uncertain tomorrow.

---

[1] This is adapted from notes of Paul Ormerod, in which he said: 'I am fundamentally in agreement with Hayek when he wrote: "an economist who is only an economist cannot be a good economist" '. The notes are available at http://rwer.wordpress.com/2010/01/21/the-lse-debate-ormerod-and-hodgson.

In this respect, McCloskey's (1983) exhortation of the broad and every-day human values of 'honesty, tolerance and clarity' is aligned with the Civil Service Code[2] and is a better guide for GES practitioners than dogged adherence to, say, a set of axiomatic rules for theoretic consistency. What is *certainly* wrong and unscientific is to defend one's own field relent-lessly with hostility to other approaches: the antithesis of a dynamic self-critical discipline that is genuinely seeking to discover new and better ways of understanding the world.

Something that practical practitioners do come to learn from expe-rience is that all economic models have shortcomings in practice, and so the emphasis on a pluralistic approach and on humility, from all the contributors to this volume, is really encouraging. Economists frequently come across in the media, and sometimes even within our own journals, as having a self-belief that is wholly unjustified by the current state of eco-nomic knowledge. Surely the reality is that there is still a great deal that reasonable people can, and do, sensibly disagree about? We do not always live up to our own ideals, but humility will help us revisit and reassess our own advice, to be self-critical and to reach for deeper understandings of our own confusions, listen to challenges and respond pragmatically to events.

I suspect that it is also the view of the majority of economists that in developing the subject we should not seek to eject any of the major building blocks from practical economics. Although all should be utilized with caution, each provides some useful insights in terms of understand-ing where the economy is and what we might do about it. Here I am thinking about concepts including opportunity cost, cost–benefit analy-sis, the IS/LM model, the Philips curve and the banking and credit system, for example. I agree with Adair Turner's emphasis that 'really good eco-nomic thinking must provide multiple partial insights, based on varied analytical approaches'.[3] And perhaps it is to misunderstand the nature of democratic society to think that all current controversies can have definitive technical 'solutions'. I do believe, however, that mainstream economics has a powerful core that is worth persisting with, and that we should do this within an approach of constant critical challenge that does not get too hooked on any particular model. We do need a toolkit but we should use it with scepticism, and we need to learn from other disciplines not just attempt to take them over. Crisis provides us with

---

[2]See www.civilservice.gov.uk/about/values.

[3]This quote is taken from a presentation at the 2010 GES Conference.

the impetus to explore alternatives that may have seemed unnecessary in more 'certain' times, and there *are* new insights (such as those from network theory) that genuinely promise new and fruitful approaches to economics. This endeavour should be carried forward with an emphasis on the transparency of assumptions and results and their shortcomings.

So I thoroughly support the consensus from the contributors to this volume that there should be a bigger role for understanding of economic thought, economic history and finance, integrated with the core economic principles of 'workhorse' courses.

What of the role of teaching and teachers in producing pragmatic and thoughtful economists for the GES or for other employers? Many previous discussions about economics degrees have focussed on preparing students to enter academia as researchers, but the reality is that most students are looking for jobs outside academia: in the media, in finance, as entrepreneurs, and of course in the public sector. For example, both the current cabinet secretary and the previous one are trained economists. So we need to provide for economists who are not destined for academia as well—and their requirements will be quite different.

Vicky Pryce, my former colleague as joint head of the GES, has stressed that economists who can say only that 'things are difficult and complex' will not be invited back by a CEO or a minister (Pryce 2011). Hence, even within a more pluralistic and sceptical approach, we do need to teach economists how to come to a reasoned judgment: practitioners do not usually have the luxury of simply concluding that 'more research is required'. Also, as the survey of the GES by Paul Anand and Jonathan Leape confirms (see chapter 3 of this book), a lot of what GES economists do is briefing for senior officials and, ultimately, for ministers. Good communication, especially with non-economists, is therefore just as vital as the need to challenge ourselves and others. To be effective as an adviser in government one has to communicate clearly and concisely to very busy people. One also has to be directly relevant to their agenda in a timely way, as well as understanding the wider political economy of policy advice.

This set of requirements has already been codified. Paragraph 2.3 of the Higher Education Quality Assurance Agency's subject benchmark for economics provides a good description of what the GES asks its members to do.[4] The best graduates can certainly do what this benchmark 'promises' but judging from the 50% of graduate applicants who fail at the GES Economic Assessment Centres (all of whom are holding or are predicted to

---

[4] Available at www.qaa.ac.uk/Publications/InformationAndGuidance/Documents/Economics.pdf.

obtain a 2:1 or better), the GES would like to see more emphasis in under-graduate degrees on a deep understanding of the threshold concepts of economics, so that graduates are better at transferring and applying these to new and unfamiliar topics. A broad quantitative competency, including descriptive statistics, is also generally more useful within the GES than a narrow training in advanced econometrics, as useful as econometrics can be. Some academics also seem to prefer to teach highly abstract technical subjects, such as advanced game theory, and perhaps this is at the expense of building proficiency in more fundamental applications. For example, cost–benefit analysis in its various manifestations—such as options appraisal, business cases and impact assessments—is used frequently right across government, but it has regrettably fallen out of many degree syllabuses. Of course, the crisis has brought home the fact that the Treasury does need experts in the role of finance in the economy, with an appreciation of its fragility. Lastly, it was a near-unanimous conclusion of the conference participants that economists will be made worldlier and less arrogant by studying aspects of economic history, particularly by focusing on approaches that highlight the shifting of perspectives and the many past mistakes of economic policy.

The GES wishes to encourage those universities that are actively addressing employers' need for economists who can exercise good judgment in their critical assessment of analysis and evidence, including from interdisciplinary sources, and who can then communicate this to a wide range of audiences. A good example is the new LSE100 course at the London School of Economics (see chapter 21). This is compulsory for all undergraduates and is aimed at producing graduates who have these skills. For similar reasons I have always valued accessible publications such as the *Oxford Review of Economic Policy* and, more recently, websites such as VoxEU. These are invaluable for their combination of excellent communication and intellectual challenge. The wide range of blogs from major economists is another new and invaluable source for the professional practitioner, and indeed for all economists. With the new debates about, for example, incorporating social impacts into cost–benefit analysis, economics will continue to evolve, as the Institute for Fiscal Studies Green Budget demonstrates in this particular example. We will need to sustain this in response to the professional challenges we face.

NEXT STEPS

This volume is a contribution to a very positive approach to changing the teaching of economics, rather than a defence of the old ways of doing

7

things. It is important for economics and its practitioners to harness this momentum, and also to take some risks. We must take strong and innovative next steps, both general ones and specific ones. For the GES, general next steps include the need to raise our game on communication and engagement with the wider academic community.

We also need to coordinate with a wide range of other employers to produce a much better articulation of the general needs of employers. The GES, and its sister profession in government, the Government Social Research profession, is also liaising with the Higher Education Funding Council for England to make the introduction of the Research Excellence Framework, with its recognition of 'impact', a success. In this respect it will be important that we work closely with our partners to ensure that we give credit where it is due to the academic influences that have helped shape our policies, while being careful to acknowledge that there may have been critical challenges to any advice we do actually finally incorporate into policies. Within the GES we are also putting a greater emphasis on transparency. This in turn encourages greater contestability, both formally through institutions such as the Office for Budget Responsibility and more informally through encouraging a more pluralistic and challenging culture and discourse.

In terms of specifics, a steering group—drawn from across academia, employers and social science practitioners—will take the momentum of the conference and this volume forward, seeking also to improve connections between high-end science and the engineering policy sharp end.

My hope is that this effort will be looked back on as another positive step in revisiting and rebalancing our discipline, but more importantly in our application of it as economists across Mankiw's whole spectrum.

Finally, we will take this effort forward with real appetite and conviction. There is a strong basis for this in the GES and in the Civil Service. There are some examples—like the economic analysis that underpinned the United Kingdom's decision on euro membership—that show we can implement successful evidence-based policies from the science end to the engineering end of economics, engaging with academics and communicating the findings clearly. We can build on this with humility, learning profound lessons from the continuing crisis.

References

Mankiw, N. G. 2006. The macroeconomist as scientist and engineer. NBER Working Paper 12349. Available at www.nber.org/papers/w12349.

McCloskey, D. N. 1983. The rhetoric of economics. *Journal of Economic Literature* 21(2):481–517.

Pryce, V. 2011. *The Dismal Science? Is Economics Influential Enough in Government Decision Making?* Institute of Government. Available at www.institutefor government.org.uk/sites/default/files/publications/The%20dismal%20scien ce.pdf.

What Makes a Good Economist?

By David Colander

Any time I think I have an even semi-profound thought about economics, all I need do is look at the history of economic thought to rid myself of such hubris. Almost inevitably I find that my thought has been said more profoundly and more elegantly by earlier economists—often by John Maynard Keynes. I am reminded of that humbling reality in trying to answer the question posed in the title of this chapter.

Keynes (1925) provided what I think of as the perfect answer to this question:

> The study of economics does not seem to require any specialised gifts of an unusually high order. Is it not, intellectually regarded, a very easy subject compared with the higher branches of philosophy and pure science? Yet good, or even competent, economists are the rarest of birds. An easy subject, at which very few excel! The paradox finds its explanation, perhaps, in that the master-economist must possess a rare *combination* of gifts. He must reach a high standard in several different directions and must combine talents not often found together. He must be mathematician, historian, statesman and philosopher—in some degree. He must understand symbols and speak in words. He must contemplate the particular in terms of the general, and touch abstract and concrete in the same flight of thought. He must study the present in the light of the past for the purposes of the future. No part of man's nature or his institutions must lie entirely outside his regard. He must be purposeful and disinterested in a simultaneous mood: as aloof and incorruptible as an artist, yet sometimes as near the earth as a politician.

The key to Keynes's insight is that he recognized that being a good economist requires a multitude of skills, and one of those skills is an ability to combine the other skills together in just the right way for the particular problem you are trying to solve. There is no set recipe: it changes with the problem, the audience and the time.

Keynes's insight—that it is the blending of skills, not the particular skills themselves, that is essential for making a good economist—makes

11

answering the second theme of this conference—what is wrong with economics education?—almost impossible. In some ways there is nothing wrong with economics education; in other ways there is lots wrong. It all depends.

This 'it depends' attitude of mine does not set well with many self-described heterodox economists, who generally argue that what is wrong with mainstream economics is that it is too mathematical; modern mainstream economics has forgotten about economic history, about economic institutions, the history of thought and methodological issues. Thus, they argue that we need to incorporate those specialties back into the curriculum to 'right' economics.

While I agree that those specialties tend to get too little focus in modern economics, I am not so sure that adding them back into the curriculum is the right solution. There are two reasons for this.

The first is that, to my mind, the problem is not that economics is too mathematical; it is that the mathematics we use in economics is way too simple to capture the complexities of economic interrelationships (see Colander *et al.* 2009). To understand the economy, an economist must understand how complex nonlinear systems of heterogeneous agents operate so that he is not overly impressed by simple linear dynamic models. To analyse complex nonlinear systems economists need more mathematics training, not less. Structuring the training of economics around a mathematical core helps strengthen students' analytical powers. The logical facilities and careful reasoning that follow from training in mathematics and in the applied mathematical techniques that economists learn serves economists well.

The second reason I am not convinced by the argument that we can improve economic training by adding more history of thought, study of institutions and economic history to the undergraduate curriculum is that teaching these specialties well generally requires great subtlety. It is not clear to me that by adding these fields back into economics, students will come away with the subtleties that a historian such as Lord Skidelsky brings to the study of Keynes, that an economist such as Charles Goodhart brings to the study of economics institutions, or that a historian of economic thought such as Mark Blaug brings to the study of the history of economic doctrines. In my view, good economists have not forgotten the broader issues—they are too obviously important to forget. Just because their graduate training does not include issues does not (or at least should not) mean that economists do not study them on their own, or recognize their importance. The formal economics curriculum is simply part of an economist's training.

I suspect that the fields of history of thought and economic history faded from economics pedagogy in large part because of the difficulties of teaching the subtleties of these fields, not because of any conscious decision by the profession to deem them unimportant. The problem is that when these subjects are taught by lesser mortals—even those who are extraordinarily bright—the subtlety of the information conveyed is often lost. I recall a history of thought class that consisted of a professor reading the manuscript of his book to the class, and an economic history class that consisted of making sure that I had memorized dates and events. I would not wish that on any student.[1]

But, you say, this time it will be different. I suspect not. In fact, I suspect that we will do worse. History of thought, economic history and the study of institutions have not been seriously taught in economics graduate programmes for decades, so it is unclear to me who would teach these courses even if they were added to the undergraduate curriculum. The point I am making is that the pedagogy question is a constrained optimization question—how can we best teach economics with the economists we have and the skills those economists possess. What we should teach needs to reflect both what we can most effectively teach and what students can learn on their own, not what we would teach in some hypothetical world. What we teach does not necessarily reflect all of what we believe students should know.

So how do we decide what economists should do and what economists should teach? My answer is that we do it locally, not globally. Each professor decides what he or she should do, and each department decides what should be taught. The reason I favour this local solution is for precisely the same reason that Keynes describes above when discussing what makes a good economist. It is a combination of skills that makes a great economist, and most of us have at best one or two skills that have sufficient gravitas to warrant saying something. It is these areas that we can teach most effectively and we should simply guide students in the other courses. In some ways, then, I have toyed with the idea that, given the existing structure of the economics profession, for those departments that want to include history of thought, methodology and economic

---

[1] Of course, there were great classes as well. Sitting in on a lecture by Amartya Sen on anything—be it the subtleties of the mathematics of social choice theory or the integration of philosophy and economics—was as close to intellectual pedagogical heaven as one can get.

history as part of the curriculum, a national group of economists should provide a reading list of books and articles that any reasonable economist would have read. Programmes that want to include these specialties could give their students this reading list and the national group could provide a yearly comprehensive exam on it.

Setting up a curriculum involves blending the skills of the available faculty to both guide and teach. It will depend critically on knowing about the specific skills available among the faculty, and the only people who can figure out how to blend them are those teaching in a particular institution. That is why general pronouncements on how undergraduate economics should be taught were avoided in my 2009 reflection of economic curriculum problems in the United States (Colander and McGoldrick 2009). In my view what needs to be taught can only be decided by the boots on the ground, not in castles in the air.

There is no general top-down formula to my laissez faire approach to the curriculum, just two provisos. The first proviso is that the economists designing the curriculum have to care. Caring, to me, means being passionate about the approach you take and wanting to teach students to become as good as they can be in that approach. The second is that one teaches with humility. Humility, in my view, is the missing element in economics teaching. Humility leads us to teach our students to become scholars rather than disciples. Humility begins with recognition that no single approach is sufficient. So even as we push our students to the limits of the approach we favour, we should also be conveying to students that there is much more to economics than *our* approach. Mathematical models are not going to provide truth, but neither are historical studies, or institutional studies. In my view, if one does not teach humility about one's approach, then one is not teaching it well. My ideal curriculum is therefore one in which teachers passionately teach the approach and specialty that they know, but they teach it with humility. Humility underlies the 'blend' aspect of economics that Keynes highlighted, and if economics trains blendable economists, economics will have less wrong with it.

REFERENCES

Colander, D., and K. McGoldrick. 2009. *Educating Economists.* Edward Elgar.
Colander, D., A. Kirman, H. Follmer, B. Sloth, K. Juselius, A. Haas and T. Lux. 2009. Mathematics, methods, and modern economics. *Real-World Economics Review*, Issue 50 (September).
Keynes, J. M. 1925. Alfred Marshall, 1842–1924. In *Memorials of Alfred Marshall* (ed. A. C. Pigou), p. 12. London: Macmillan.

What Economists Do—And How Universities Might Help

By Paul Anand and Jonathan Leape

A famous definition, due to Jacob Viner, is that 'economics is what economists do'. A natural question to ask, then, is, what is it that they do? We know something about what academic economists do, but we know *much* less about what professional economists do—what it is to be an economics practitioner. A small number of articles, published mainly in American Economic Association journals, give occasional snapshots from a US perspective (see, for example, Stiglitz 1998) but the apparent flourishing of the discipline in the United Kingdom as a trade embodying valuable skills has until now not be given the attention we feel it merits. To right this egregious wrong, we have been collaborating with the Government Economic Service to design a survey of its members that would contribute to our understanding of what central government economists do, how they go about it and what might be the implications, if there are any, for teachers and researchers in the university sector. We shall be sharing the survey results of this work with the profession more widely in a future publication (Anand and Leape 2012) but we take the opportunity here to comment particularly on some of the initial findings. We consider their implications for the design of university curricula intended to equip people for a career in which economics is used to shape and guide public policy.

In January 2012 we surveyed members of the United Kingdom's Government Economic Service, receiving nearly 500 responses[1] from across

The authors are particularly grateful to all the members of the Government Economic Service who were kind enough to reply to our survey, to Andy Ross, its Deputy Director, who helped us develop the survey, to the Royal Economics Society for support via its small project grant programme, and to Erina Ytsma for excellent research assistance. We also thank Diane Coyle for organizing the meeting at the Bank of England where some of these results were first aired.

[1] A response rate of approximately 25%, which is high for many kinds of organizational survey.

the full range of central government departments and the Bank of England. Economics plays a key role in central government decision making. The survey sought to identify the principal activities, methods and approaches, the use of research and training, and the areas of economics that are used by economists in government in the United Kingdom. In this short overview, we discuss some of the lessons that emerge, focusing on questions relating to the type of work done and methods used and on the open-ended question, 'Are there any changes in your university economics training that would better prepare you as a professional economist in government?'

We highlight several of the most prominent themes to emerge. This may shed light on how economists contribute to the work of government, and at the same time provide some constructive suggestions for designers of university courses aimed at supporting public policy analysis. As the Government Economic Service is currently the largest single employer of graduate economists in the United Kingdom, these themes and suggestions—which are of most direct relevance to the preparation of economists working in the public sector—should be of some interest. Moreover, it seems likely that the themes that are relevant to (applied) economists in the public sector will also be germane to the training of private sector economists (and hence be of relevance to most university courses).

Perhaps the most striking finding, even if it is an obvious one, is that what economists do is in some sense to *apply* their economics training. In answer to the open-ended question, the single most dominant theme was reflected in comments such as 'Greater focus on practical application', albeit with some variation in what was meant by 'application'. To unpack this a little more, some respondents stressed the importance of using a range of practical examples while teaching: of ways in which externalities could be countered, for instance. Sometimes, these examples could be considered to be topics (like public economics) or methods (such as cost–benefit analysis) in their own right. A particularly noteworthy comment was made by a respondent who made a comparison with the need for being trained in how to drive a car and not how to build one.

This point is reinforced by evidence from the survey that the two dominant areas of work for these economists is the 'production of briefing material' and the preparation of 'policy advice'—tasks performed by 75% and 70% of all our respondents, respectively. Moreover, in terms of approaches and methods, 'synthesizing evidence' was clearly the most important, cited by 84% of respondents. Interestingly, these results hold for economists holding postgraduate degrees in economics as well as for those holding only undergraduate degrees. Indeed, the dominant importance of synthesizing evidence is even more pronounced among postgraduates.

Reorienting teaching towards application may require some thought about what it is to apply knowledge in the economics field. Courses that were given specific mentions included one on 'regional economics' and another on 'economics in government', both of which originated in Scotland as it happened. Although there is considerable interest in developing training around the application of economic theory, it is worth recognizing that the skills developed and the areas of theory drawn on may change. And the making a car versus driving a car analogy seems to be a particularly pertinent distinction. The application of economic tools to the evaluation of policy proposals seems to be a skill that many would welcome an opportunity to develop further at university. Such skills might be developed through the use of case studies or even through economic debates (perhaps in the style of law moots).

An increased emphasis on application also has broader potential implications. Knowledge of institutions and how they might impact on policy design as derived from contemporary economic history is likely to be an important part of this mix. So too is an approach to the use of models that emphasizes their selective use and their role not as ends in themselves but as starting points for serious empirical analysis. A deeper theme that emerges is thus a recognition, in this context, of the importance of inductive approaches as a complement to the elegant deductive economics that has tended to dominate the core teaching in economics.

This theme is evident in one respondent's use of the phrase ad hoc problem solving, which far from being a negative term highlights the particular nature of the needs of policy analysis. Effective application depends on much more than the acquisition of knowledge about underlying principles. It requires an ability to work from the bottom up: to *start* with data and to draw on a range of tools to learn from that data. The good news here is that in recent years there has been a dramatic expansion in high-quality empirical research in economics and in the range of tools available, although it is perhaps the case that more still needs to be done to integrate this into undergraduate programmes.

Unsurprisingly then, we find, in addition, a strand of comments underscoring the centrality of data to the work of policy economists. A key aspect of this relates to data gathering. Respondents highlight the need for training in a variety of topics: from the acquisition and cleansing of

17

data to the range of methods used to obtain information (survey design, focus groups, etc.). Government economists work in an environment in which answers may require the application of economic theory to information that has to be generated for the purpose in hand rather than to secondary data off the shelf. The professional economist often has to contribute to a number of judgements around data acquisition: how the data acquisition process should be designed; what questions should be asked and how should they be asked; and so on.

Such training is often provided on research methods courses provided by statisticians or quantitative social scientists, but the message we seem to be getting is that at least some government economists would be interested in such training as well. Data analysis in economics is now very much focused on the analysis of secondary data only, whereas institutions also collect a large of amount of their own data.

The comment on ad hoc problem solving mentioned above is relevant here, too. If politics is about 'stuff happening', then many of the questions that civil servants are asked will inevitably not have been foreseen by the designers of routine surveys. In any case, there is clearly an interest in a broadening out of the training that some economists receive. Beyond the demand for skills in data gathering, there seems to be a clear need for a stronger set of empirical skills aimed at learning from data—in addition to the skills, more commonly used in academic research, involved in using data to test a particular model.

A related theme concerns the use of econometrics. This emerges as an important method and as one for which, for some, more training would be desirable. Interestingly, in terms of the approaches and methods used, while just over 50% of respondents were involved in conducting or commissioning econometric analysis, more than 70% made use of published econometric analysis. These results were mirrored in the results for the areas in which additional training was deemed useful, with more than 60% of respondents valuing additional training in 'evaluating econometric work done by others', against 48% who wanted additional training in 'doing econometrics'. This suggests a clear demand for econometrics as a central part of curricula to support policy analysis, with the important caveat that *understanding and interpretation of applied econometric* work is of most relevance to this group.

Communication also emerged as an important theme. Government economists spend a considerable amount of their time developing policy briefings and this is fundamentally a job that concerns the translation of analysis conducted in the terminology of an academic discipline into words, images and stories that are intelligible to decision makers, the media and the public while remaining true to the underlying analysis. This is no mean feat, but the central role of communication comes out clearly in the results cited above, which show that the production of briefing material and policy advice are the two main aspects of the work, identified by an overwhelming 75% and 70% of respondents, respectively. The finding is reinforced by the results on additional desired training, where 'presenting economic analysis to different audiences' was identified by just over 60% of our respondents (this was ranked joint highest with the evaluation of econometric work).

In this brief overview we have tried to bring out the most important recurrent themes. In all cases, occasional counterexamples notwithstanding, the themes we highlight seem to reflect a consensus of sorts. Government economists are now distributed across all the spending departments and the quality and relevance of their university training clearly helps explain why this has happened. However, some forms of university training are clearly more relevant than others to the jobs that government economists do. One respondent suggests that graduate economists should not see themselves simply as experts but as 'having gleaned a wide range of professional skills (communication, analysis, drafting, presentation, project management, etc.)'.

We think this is potentially an important insight that underlines the fact that economists can and should develop many kinds of skills complementary to their knowledge of models and their derivation. These complementary skills, especially in the area of empirical analysis, are particularly valuable to practising economists, and some courses and pathways could usefully pay more explicit attention to their development in educational practices. One respondent suggested that members of the Government Economic Service could go out to universities and run workshops explaining how government economists think. Such knowledge exchanges could provide useful insights into how course options and approaches might be better aligned with the demands of economists in policy positions. More generally, these insights suggest a strong case for incorporating a significant element of project work and case studies into university programmes.

The themes we have discussed derive from the insights of practising economists. Inevitably, they are not a random sample of those who study economics, reflecting as they do very much a self-selected group: nonetheless, they constitute an important section of the economics community.

Their interest in the discipline is evident from the replies we received (one even wrote: 'Economics is a fantastic subject but ...'). Now that economics plays an integral role in UK policymaking, we believe that exchanges between the policy and academic worlds can enrich our understanding and experiences of economics both as a core feature of the world and as a system of thought about it.

Professional economics is clearly a distinct activity in its own right, not a watered-down version of anything else, and economics is increasingly important to the quality of people's lives. What professional economists do is apply their economics, applying some aspects more than others, and in combination with other kinds of information and institutional details relevant to the problem in hand. The term 'apply' perhaps does not do full justice to the creative and synthetic nature of this task. The competencies required are broad-ranging and worth reflecting on in thinking about the future of university programmes in economics, at both undergraduate and postgraduate level.

REFERENCES

Anand, P., and J. Leape. 2012. How economists help governments think. In preparation.

Stiglitz, J. 1998. Distinguished Lecture on Economics in Government. The private uses of public interests: incentives and institutions. *Journal of Economic Perspectives* 12(2):3–22.

Economists in the Financial Markets

By Stephen King

John Kay's description (see page 54) of a typical day in the life of an economist working in financial markets ('Business economists work in financial institutions, which principally use them to entertain their clients at lunch or advertise their banks in fillers on CNBC') may be amusing but is it close to the truth? Well, I admit to having the occasional lunch and I do spend time appearing on CNBC, Bloomberg and other such channels, but there is much more to the job than that.

Economists working within financial markets tend to have geographical specialities, as experts on the United Kingdom, the Eurozone, China, the United States and so on. They need to know the institutional arrangements of their specialist region in great depth. They need to be absolutely on top of economic data as they are released, giving instant analysis of their implications for financial markets. They have to provide analysis and forecasts, both for monthly data releases and for the outlook one, two or even five years ahead, typically in the form of monthly publications, quarterlies and one-off 'specials' on a topic of interest. And they have to present their views to the bank's clients—not all of whom will be trained economists—in a clear and intelligible way. That can entail a huge amount of international travel.

Bank economists are also very much aware that they are operating in a competitive marketplace. That means they have to act not just as writers of research but as sellers of it as well. The most valuable activities of bank economists are often associated with the consultancy services they provide: the visits to pension funds, hedge funds, insurance companies, corporate treasurers, CEOs and CFOs, alongside briefings to members of staff, where they 'sell their wares'. These meetings only happen, however, if customers are willing to give up their time and (in some cases) pay commission. Economists must therefore be able to offer genuinely valuable insight.

So what is it that bank economics teams require from would-be employees? Numeracy is certainly essential, but it is not enough simply to be numerate. Ideas have to be expressed clearly both on paper and face to face. Economists who can provide mathematical rigour alone are unlikely to be successful: clients are well aware that even the best econometric models have a nasty habit of going wrong. An ability to talk about risks within a 'big picture' framework is just as important, and mathematical rigour does not always lend itself to this imaginative approach.

That need for breadth, in turn, means that the successful financial market economist should have a range of other skills and areas of knowledge.

Knowledge of Economic History

Too few economists newly arriving in the financial world have any real knowledge of events that, while sometimes in the distant past, may have tremendous relevance for current affairs. For example, an understanding of how the gold standard operated, including its strengths and weaknesses, is helpful in analysing the Eurozone's current plight. So too is a knowledge of the Exchange Rate Mechanism crisis of 1992–93. The global financial crisis can be more easily interpreted and understood by someone who has prior knowledge about the 1929 crash, the Great Depression and, for that matter, the 1907 crash.

Admittedly, these events are not easy to analyse using modern-day mathematical and statistical techniques: the pre-computer world has its data limitations too. There is no reason, however, to limit economic understanding to what can readily be downloaded into a spreadsheet with n degrees of freedom. A more imaginative approach is required, if only to expand the mind beyond what can be immediately sliced and diced in different statistical ways. Economic history can enlighten, in particular by emphasizing the social and political forces that lead to economic booms and busts. Economists should not be slaves to economic data that reflect only the most recent experience.

International Economic Relationships

Although many financial economists specialize in one particular country or region, increasingly they are expected to analyse the impact of events in one part of the world on other regions. Higher oil prices, slowing Chinese growth, new 'south–south trade' and financial linkages all have potentially large global effects. Our clients expect us to come up with analysis to cast light on these issues. We have to be both quick and methodical. Despite our regional specialization, we cannot afford to treat each country as an island.

Domestic versus Foreign Drivers of Economic Developments

Many economic developments are misinterpreted or ignored because, too often, there is an assumption that policymakers are perfectly in control of a nation's destiny. Is inflation in the United Kingdom purely determined by the output gap—as many would-be and practising economists seem to think—or is UK inflation increasingly influenced by events beyond our shores? The so-called Great Moderation—the period of steady growth combined with low and stable inflation—was hijacked by central bankers keen to burnish their own price stability credentials; as it turns out, though, much of the drop in inflation reflected the impact of low-cost imports from the emerging world. More recently, the stickiness of higher-than-target inflation may reflect the impact of burgeoning emerging market demand for raw materials.

Financial Markets

One of the great unanswered, and sometimes unasked, questions in economics concerns the role of financial markets. Young economists arrive in the financial world with little or no knowledge of how the financial system operates. This is a matter of collective guilt. Economic models typically assume that the financial system is a black box that just so happens to work. We discovered during the financial crisis that this was hopelessly wide of the mark, but few economists had the knowledge, ability or techniques to understand properly what was going on. Economists should have a much better understanding of why, in principle, financial markets can fail and what the potential warning signs might be. Also helpful in this area—and, indeed, in plenty of others—would be a better understanding of behavioural economics and, in particular, how incentive structures can lead to undesirable outcomes.

Global Capital Flows

The growth of global capital flows was arguably the biggest revolution in international economic behaviour in the last thirty years, and yet, in the absence of detailed and reliable data, it is also one of the most poorly understood. At the very least, simple accounting principles should be instilled: for every current account surplus there must be an offsetting deficit. Too often the balance of payments is described purely in trade terms, but nowadays it is surely the capital account tail that wags the current account dog.

23

Political Economy

A spell in the civil service is always useful to enable economists to separate the politically possible from the economically desirable. At the very least, a working knowledge of the history of economic ideas is useful, if only to emphasize that the greatest economic thinkers understood the political context in which they were operating. Unfashionably normative by the recent standards of academic economics, political economy is what ultimately drives policy decisions.

Finally, I lament the fact that economists coming into the financial world struggle to relate what they have learnt at university to economic developments in the real world. I have asked recent university leavers how much time they had spent in lectures and seminars on the financial crisis. Most admitted that the subject had not even been raised. This is profoundly disappointing. Not all students will be taught during a period of genuine economic upheaval—for good or bad—but the chance to match their theoretical understanding with historic events reported all over the media is surely too good an opportunity to be dismissed so casually.

Economics: Purposes and Directions Post-Crisis

By Bridget Rosewell

What does it mean to be an economist? What is economics about? What do economists agree on? It is interesting that a discipline that appears to be powerful and important should need to ask such questions. Yet it clearly does. Most professions have charters and organizations that set standards. They require continuing professional development. Economics does not. At the conference that forms the basis of this book, no member of the audience of economists was prepared to agree that even half of the contents of the typical textbook were true!

Perhaps this is the reason that economists (I am not going to use the term profession any more) have found it difficult to respond effectively to the challenge of the financial crisis. When the Queen, opening a new building for the London School of Economics, asked her famous question about why economists did not see this coming, one answer, from London School of Economics economists, suggested it was because there were always external shocks and that models would not capture these. Another answer, from a more eclectic group of which I was part, suggested that economists had neglected the lessons of history and overplayed the possibility of prediction. A subsequent seminar at the London School of Economics, with speakers from both groups, was able to agree that economic history and the history of economic thought were undertaught and undervalued.

Both of these subjects would definitely bring a different tone and much less certainty to economics than is presently found. Greater humility about the contribution of economists might well result, and a wider range of people with different interests might be attracted to the subject. But to be able to agree that history matters does not answer the question of what economics is about. Here, I want to address the purpose of economics, the purpose of economists, and the relationships between economics and other disciplines.

These reflections are based on my own experience both in academic life and in policymaking. In macroeconomics and in competition and planning policy areas alike, there is quite a gap between economic theory, practice and reality. These gaps continue to drive my interest in doing economics differently. From being one of (former UK Chancellor of the Exchequer) Kenneth Clarke's 'seven wise men', to giving evidence as an expert witness, to working as the Chief Economist to the Mayor of London and the Greater London Assembly for eight years, to making the case for infrastructure projects, it has always been important to me to think about how economics works in practice.

THE PURPOSE OF ECONOMICS

Economics has been described as the study of resource allocation: the relationship between ends and scarce means (Robbins 1932). Much of standard microeconomics deals with this and the identification of optimal conditions for optimal allocation. Much progress has been made in considering how to create such conditions when taking into account human failings such as limited information, inadequately defined rules of the game, and so on.

These approaches have become highly influential in technical research and in government. Unfortunately, much of this does not connect with what non-economists think economics is for. In business, economics is essentially for dealing with regulators—few businesses employ economists directly to understand their markets or to analyse their decisions. If economists are employed for anything other than involvement in regulatory processes, it is to look at external events and to prepare forecasts. It is forecasting the macroeconomy that the outside world thinks economics is about. Yet in this area of economics, there is still only limited progress beyond time series curve fitting.

If economics is about understanding how economies evolve, there is indeed little to agree on. Our understanding of growth and innovation are limited (see, for example, Antonelli 2003). How institutions affect growth and performance is contested—indeed there is little available on economic dynamics and processes of adjustment. Hypotheses, theories and empirical testing all need a lot more work. So even though economics has made progress on micro matters, outsiders do not think of these as our main function.

Moreover, even in microeconomics the areas of activity that our models cover are far from complete. Economic analysis deals best with markets in which it is reasonable to assume that agents are independent and similarly informed, and in which products of consistent and unchanging quality are readily available. As the world has become more connected and products more variable, these assumptions become less and less relevant. Network and fashion effects can produce results that are very different from those that result from a standard market analysis, with heuristics, rules of thumb and winner-takes-all outcomes (two classic references are Schelling (1973) and Watts (2002)). The description of the rational agent in a world with choice overload might be very different from the description of such an agent in a world with limited choice and with the ability to collect all relevant information. To be complete, economics needs to deal with all possibilities.

Years ago, I conducted a study whose aim was to measure marginal and average cost curves to assess whether a product was being dumped.[1] The managers of the factories I visited found these concepts to be bizarre. All the relationships were full of discontinuities and managerial trade-offs. The main difference between plants was between the quality of their management and the shop floor relationships. Forcing costs into the predefined models was like forcing my feet into high heels: painful and likely to result in an accident.

I therefore conclude that different people are likely to believe different things about the purpose of economics, and even in the context of a narrow definition focusing on the allocation of resources, we have still only scratched the surface. In terms of a wider definition that covers the evolution of the economy, growth, dynamics and innovation, we are much further away from a consensus about economics.

THE PURPOSE OF ECONOMISTS

What are economists for? A cynic might believe that their purpose is to think up rules. Indeed, many economists in public policy circles certainly do this, in competition cases and in regulated industries, for example. They work on the basis that they must try to make the industry in question as much like a perfect market as possible. Many appear not to have heard of the fundamental theorem of second best—established over fifty years ago by Lipsey and Lancaster (1956–57)—which says that making one industry 'perfect' might make the system less so.

Nevertheless, there is plenty of employment in categorizing an industry, defining its degree of competition and modelling what it might look like—and there is plenty of scope for disagreement too, which adds to the employment prospects for economists. The concepts in use are those

---

[1] The study was for the National Economic Development Office and it looked at the production of television sets.

that focus on the equilibrium output of an industry when there is profit maximization. Of course, this leaves out the possibility that equilibrium might not be useful in a changing industry, and that maximization is nearly impossible too.

It could be that we need people to 'think like an economist'. I define this as considering incentives, balancing costs and benefits, and asking about market failures. This is certainly the contribution of economics in public policy. Perhaps it should also be about wanting to look at the data. Economic data did not exist before there were economists. Adam Smith relied on case studies and descriptions. No Standard Industrial Classification, no price indices, no output statistics. Much of the work of economic historians is trying to patch together the data needed to do economics as it is practised today.

However, it is quite surprising how little economists know about the data they use and how much they take for granted. I have heard economists complain that market data—of the number of telephone calls made, for example—is too 'soft' compared with data on employment levels. Yet estimates of employment in London differ by as much as 200,000 people between different data sources. Economic data gets revised, is estimated on the basis of samples, and tries to measure the hard-to-measure. Market data is clear, is never revised, and measures just what it says it measures. The problem lies in interpreting it. Economists think they understand economic data because they have been taught a concept. Whether the statistic measures that concept is a whole other story, and one that needs a lot more attention. Thinking like an economist should include knowing the nuts and bolts of the numbers.

The purpose of an economist might be to understand how the economy works. I have to say that after forty years of trying I still find huge puzzles here. What is the most effective balance between tradeables and non-tradeables? How do we define a 'local' economy? When does turning non-marketed activity into marketed activity undermine civil society? What is the right way to compensate those affected by the destruction part of creative destruction? How is risk managed and what can economists say about this?

There are about 1,500 economists in government service in the United Kingdom. The habits of thought that an economist learns can indeed be very useful in government: looking at costs as well as benefits is an obvious example. The skills of number crunching and of the use of logic and rationality can be useful. But some ways of 'economics thinking' can be less helpful, including believing that the economist's world view is perfect, that maximizing rational behaviour is possible, and that the data are correct.

CAN ECONOMICS LEARN FROM OTHER DISCIPLINES?

Economists are often accused of having physics envy: of wanting to be too scientific, too mathematics-oriented. Indeed, the standard neoclassical model can be aligned to the standard Newtonian physical model, where there are no uncertainties and the laws have predictable consequences.

However, the scientific method—according to which hypotheses are tested against data and must then be replicated and retested before being accepted—is a good starting point for any form of enquiry. Of course, we know that experiment is hard in social science. It is in medicine as well, but the double blind trial has still been developed and tested in the medical field to ensure that treatments do work.

A rigorous approach to the testing of hypotheses and an open mind are good precursors to creating an established discipline. Anthropology is an example of a discipline that was troubled, at the outset, by evidence collection that appeared to find what it was looking for, and it had its fair share of scandals. Over time, professionalization and evidence standard-ization have contributed to significant improvements in the reliability of its results. Psychology too has gathered a body of confirmed evidence and supported hypotheses, and these have resulted in the discipline making inroads into economics.

Economics has seen itself as the most scientific of the social sciences. Nonetheless, some of its key hypotheses about agent behaviour have been undermined by experiments about actual decision making. It is time to take a good look at how to extend the coverage of the subject to the nature of rationality, to how agents are connected and influence each other, and to the processes of economic growth and evolution.

Of course, there are circumstances in which the standard model of inde-pendent market participants, able on average to build a good model of the market in a rational way, will be a sensible approach. But there are many circumstances in which these conditions will not hold. It was noteworthy that innovation, growth and disruption were little discussed at the con-ference that was the origin of this book. What is the model for considering large-scale investment that will change connectivity between markets, for example? What about technical innovation that disrupts markets? These are the sorts of changes that have been a distinguishing feature of cap-italism and that have made possible the high standard of living and the good health and longevity we now enjoy. We did not discuss these and we must.

Businesses are all about processes and how to make better decisions, or indeed any decisions. The decisions they do make are likely to have consequences in the real world, which in turn have consequences for other businesses. An understanding of this and how behaviour and motivation might matter for outcomes is an important area that will not be captured by equilibrium analysis.

Moreover, if most ordinary people think economics is about forecasting, then analysis of the limits of predictability is also crucial, as is explaining the limitations to the wider public.

Students need to be taught about the history of the subject and its limitations as well as the exciting challenges that await them in a discipline that is rich in good problems to get one's teeth into.

In summary, economics continues to have good problems, and some of the skills it teaches are powerful. But it still lacks a set of good theories and quite often lacks good data as well.

References

Antonelli, C. 2003. *The Economics of Innovation, New Technologies, and Structural Change.* Oxford: Routledge.

Lipsey, R. G., and K. Lancaster. 1956–57. The general theory of second best. *Review of Economic Studies* 24(1):11–32.

Robbins, L. 1932. *An Essay on the Nature and Significance of Economic Science.* London: Macmillan.

Schelling, T. C. 1973. Hockey helmets, concealed weapons, and daylight saving: a study of binary choices with externalities. *Journal of Conflict Resolution* 17: 381–428.

Watts, D. J. 2002. A simple model of global cascades on random networks. *Proceedings of the National Academy of Sciences of the USA* 99(9):5766–5771.

The Importance of Communicating Post-Crisis Economics

By Steve Schifferes

The global financial crisis has presented both a challenge and an opportunity to the economics profession. Economists have been accused—by no less than Her Majesty the Queen, among others—of failing to predict the crisis. Their complex mathematical models of the economy are now under attack for being unable to explain how the failure of a single US investment bank precipitated a serious world economic downturn.

The new debate among economists, which focuses less on economic modelling and more on the linkages between the financial sector and the rest of the economy, is a welcome return to an older tradition in economics that was much more plugged into practical policymaking. But such a paradigm shift may take some time to reach conclusions—and meanwhile the crisis is far from over.

At the same time, the continuing crisis has provided an enormous opportunity for the economics profession to reach out to the public.

There has been intense public interest in the state of the economy since 2008, and polling commissioned by City University London has shown that people are following the news about the economic crisis very closely (Schifferes 2012). Many people are also seeking a deeper explanation of the crisis and its trajectory, and they feel they have not been well served by the media. If there was ever a moment when economics could make an impact on popular understanding, it is now.

WHAT THE AUDIENCE WANTS

In any attempt at communication, the first step is to understand who the audience is and what it wants. Economists have traditionally focused on communicating with other academics through journals and conferences, and reaching out to policymakers through private meetings and opinion pieces. Interacting with the general public has not been a high priority for most of them. The challenge for the economics profession now is to bring its expertise to the public debate.

Right now there is a ready-made audience for such efforts. The majority of the public are following the crisis closely or very closely, with more than half looking at news about the economy daily or several times a day. Our survey showed that nearly half the population feel they do not fully understand the nature of the crisis and how it might impinge on their own lives. Even more believe they have not been given an adequate explanation by the media. People are naturally particularly interested in the things that impact on their daily lives: jobs, their standard of living and cutbacks in government spending.

However, it should be remembered that the public has only a very hazy understanding of even basic economic concepts: concepts such as gross domestic product, bond yields and interest rates. Any use of jargon is likely to turn off a large proportion of the audience.

In addition, the policy debate about what to do to prevent future crises has not penetrated very deeply into the public consciousness. Instead, people are attributing blame for the crisis to particular groups, such as bankers and politicians, implying that it was personal moral failings rather than systemic structural problems that were the cause of the crisis. There is even less understanding of the way the financial system was regulated in the past, and how that might change in the future.

WHAT JOURNALISTS NEED: A GOOD STORY AND RELIABLE SOURCES

Economists will have to work through the media to get their message across in order to inform the public debate. Yet the relationship between economists and journalists has not always been an easy one, especially in the United Kingdom. Many economists feel that the media often trivializes issues, and they are afraid that their comments will be distorted or reported inaccurately. Economic journalists complain that it is often very difficult to get academic economists to comment on current developments. But both journalists and economists have a lot to contribute to each other.

What economic journalists need above all is a reliable source: someone they can turn to when a crisis breaks, or when they are trying to develop some original insights into an ongoing story. This is not just a matter of the level of intellectual insight that can be brought to the subject: it is also a matter of recognizing the needs of journalists, who are working under extreme time pressure and often need to fit comments into an existing narrative in order to interest their editor.

So in order to engage in the debate, economists will have to consider sacrificing one of their most valuable commodities—time—and make a conscious choice to engage in the debate at least initially in the terms along which it has already developed. This requires a degree of commitment that not everyone in the economics profession is prepared to make.

For those who are prepared to make the commitment, though, the reward could be the creation of a deeper relationship with a limited number of key economic correspondents. The advantage for the journalist is that they have someone they can turn to who they know will respond to their requests. The advantage for the economist is that they have a ready and hopefully responsive audience for their own research agenda.

Getting coverage in the media requires more than contacts. It also requires the ability to tell a story, to pitch an idea in a narrative form, and to make it relevant to people's lives and the current policy debate.

To start with, economists have to know what the essence of their argument is and how to summarize it succinctly. If you cannot give a one-sentence summary of the point you are trying to make, you are unlikely to get much coverage. The one-sentence version is an essential prelude to longer and more sophisticated versions. Secondly, the approach must be free of jargon and touch lightly, if at all, on the mathematics of theoretical models. Numeracy—among the public and indeed among some journalists—cannot be assumed. Thirdly, to get a hearing at all the argument must be couched in terms of a current policy or political debate. It is both a challenge and an opportunity to be relevant as well as original and rigorous. Fourthly, and most importantly, the pitch must find a way of making its argument relevant to ordinary people. It is the human examples that make stories come alive and turn them into a compelling piece of reading that will attract the attention of the audience.

It should be remembered that all good journalism is essentially storytelling. The narrative—influenced as it is by argument, debate and case studies—is all, and the journalist cannot reach his or her audience without it. And while it is up to the journalist to supply such a narrative, the economist can be an essential collaborator in this task.

REFOCUSING THE DEBATE

There are three areas in which post-crisis economics can make a significant contribution to refocusing the public debate.

Firstly, the new emphasis among economists on the importance of understanding history, and particularly the history of economic crises, can provide a powerful tool for public understanding. Looking at the narrative of past events, and drawing some lessons for the present, is an effective way of illuminating and perhaps clarifying current debates. It also helps people engage, whether they have personal experience of such past events or just a broad sense of economic history. Of course, all history is contested, and there will be differences among economists about what those lessons are, whether they apply to the Great Depression of the 1930s, the Japanese 'lost decade' of the 1990s or the Argentine devaluation of 2001. But without examining history, it will be harder to understand or predict the outcome of the current crisis.

A second element in post-crisis economics also provides a convenient handle to engage the public. This is the re-emergence in economics of an emphasis on the importance of institutions, including how they came to be as they are, as key to understanding the crisis. Again, this takes the crisis from the general to the particular, looking at specific relationships such as the structure of the banking sector, the particular form of regulation, and the different responses of central banks across different regimes. The differing responses to the global crisis in different countries suggest that this will be a fruitful line of investigation, and one which can also have its own narrative, bringing together economic, political and cultural factors.

Thirdly, the shift in economic thinking from theoretical models to a more policy-focused approach, examining the regulatory response to the crisis, puts the economics profession back in the heart of the policy debate. However, explaining this to the public is still a hard sell, as it lacks a convincing narrative, such as emerged in the 1930s in the United States when the Pecora Commission galvanized the public. These Senate hearings—which confronted bankers and publicized the mis-selling and insider dealing of the 1920s—led directly to the adoption of tighter regulation, including the creation of the Securities and Exchange Commission and the Glass–Steagall Act, which separated investment and retail banking.

There is no doubt that the issue of regulation is more complex now, in terms of both the range of instruments being considered and the difficulty of regulating at a national level in a globalized financial system. However, it is not unreasonable to wonder if some of the obfuscation is deliberate, if only because policymakers are not sure how the public would react to the news that the Bank of England now has the right to limit their access to mortgages and order drastic cutbacks in credit, or because the financial sector sees an advantage in a certain lack of clarity. But without widespread public support the regulators are facing an effective push-back from the far-from-moribund banking sector. Telling the regulatory story to the public via the media is therefore important.

Finally, one has to wonder how much the debate on post-crisis economics will turn into a debate about the role of the market in our society. All of the above perspectives imply that there are limits to the free operation of markets, shaped by history, institutions and governments. This is a significant change from the tone of pre-crisis policy debate. There is already a lively discussion among other social scientists about the ethical dimensions of the role of markets (see, for example, Sandel 2012) and whether the assumption of a rational economic man corresponds with the psychological reality (set out in Kahneman (2011)). Some of this, especially behavioural economics, has already been taken up by the economics profession and has been applied to the crisis. But in some ways it is surprising—especially in light of the failure of much economic modelling to predict the crisis—that the debate on 'market fundamentalism' has not had a greater resonance within the economics community itself.

Making an Impact: The Role of Public Intellectuals

Communicating complex economic ideas is quite challenging, even with the cooperation of journalists. Few economists have wanted to engage with the public, venturing into often unfamiliar territory with uncertain results.

However, it would be a serious mistake if, as a result of the crisis, the profession retreated even further into its ivory tower.

First of all, there are now serious economic issues at stake that will affect everyone. Engaging in that debate about how we shape the future—and understand where we are going—is something that should concern us all.

Secondly, we are still struggling to understand how far we can limit the risks of future crises by changes in regulation and government action. This debate will be strengthened by holding it in public, so that all the players—and the public—can participate openly. Any changes that are made without such a full debate are likely to lack legitimacy and be short lived.

Thirdly, opening up the discussion can serve as a reality check on the development of more complex and theoretical mathematical models, which may not do a very good job in helping understand the real world.

Finally, there is an equity argument. As taxpayers have supported economic research, they need to see the results and understand its usefulness if such support is to continue in hard times. This is the essence of looking for 'impact' in tax-funded research.

Underlying this discussion is a broader issue: namely, what role the academy should play in the wider polity. Despite the urging of the research councils, the academic community in the United Kingdom has often been quite reluctant to engage with the big policy debates of the day. This is in contrast to the situation in the United States, where a number of economists, from both left and right (such as Paul Krugman and Joseph Stiglitz on the left, and Glenn Hubbard and Martin Feldstein on the right), have taken a prominent role in the public debate. The relative lack of such public intellectuals in the United Kingdom has made it more difficult to fashion a coherent response to the crisis, and has left the field open for more self-interested parties to shape public opinion, be they financiers, governments or the media itself.

REFERENCES

Kahneman, D. 2011. *Thinking, Fast and Slow*. Allen Lane.

Sandel, M. 2012. *What Money Can't Buy: The Moral Limits of Markets*. Allen Lane.

Schifferes, S. 2012. Trust-meltdown for business journalism. *British Journalism Review* 23(2):55–60.

PART 2

ECONOMIC METHODOLOGY AND IMPLICATIONS FOR TEACHING

What Post-Crisis Changes Does the Economics Discipline Need? Beware of Theory Envy!

By Andrew W. Lo

During my first week as a graduate student in economics, I attended a pleasant social event organized by the senior students in the department: a Saturday evening party that was meant to help first-year students ease into the demanding programme. I sat down among a group of fourth-year students and they kindly offered to give me the lay of the land regarding the challenges of the first-year curriculum. After several beers they began to talk more expansively about economics and economists. One student said, 'if you took all the economists in the world and laid them end to end, they'd never reach a conclusion'. Another student added, 'economists have forecasted five out of the past three recessions'. A third student claimed that President Harry S. Truman once asked for a one-armed economist to serve as his advisor and when asked why, Truman replied: 'So he can't say "on the one hand, but on the other hand"'. But the story I remember best was told by a graduating student who had worked as a research assistant for the head of the Council of Economic Advisors—a prestigious position that gave him unique insights into how economic policy was formulated. His story was about the glory days of the former Soviet Union, when the military would hold a parade each year to celebrate May Day, and leading the procession of tanks, missiles and bazooka-bearing infantry marching proudly towards Red Square was a row of goose-stepping economists. One spectator turned to his companion and asked: 'Comrade, why are there economists marching in this military parade?' His friend replied: 'Comrade, do you have any idea how much damage they can do?!'

I thank Diane Coyle for giving me the opportunity to contribute a pre-conference essay, and Jerry Chafkin, Doyne Farmer, Paul Mende, Bob Merton and Mark Mueller for many stimulating discussions over the years on this topic. The views and opinions expressed in this article are those of the author only and do not necessarily represent the views and opinions of AlphaSimplex, the Bank of England, Enlightenment Economics, the UK Government Economic Service, MIT, any of their affiliates or employees, or any of the individuals acknowledged above.

Were these jokes funny? I suppose you had to be there. From my under-graduate economics classes, I had an idea about what the other students were alluding to: the imprecision of economic forecasts, the raging debate among leading economists regarding the effectiveness of monetary pol-icy, and the unintended consequences of regulation and policy interven-tions. I knew all of these things, but I presumed that the more advanced economics courses I was about to take would go beyond these limitations. I was dead wrong. After a semester of graduate-level microeconomics, macroeconomics and econometrics, I came to the depressing realization that most of what I had heard at that cocktail party were not, in fact, jokes. At best, they were examples of gallows humour by economists who knew all too well how inexact a 'science' economics really was. At the end of that first semester, I started filling out applications for law school.

I will describe what saved me from that ignominious fate later, but the uneasiness I felt as a graduate student was apparently more wide-spread than I had appreciated back then. The seeds of conflict in eco-nomics had been sown decades earlier by visionaries and iconoclasts such as Thorstein Veblen, Joseph Schumpeter, Maurice Allais, John May-nard Keynes and, most notably, Herbert Simon: a well-respected mathe-matical economist who abandoned the field of economics in the 1950s to study human behaviour using computer simulations and psychology. Often acknowledged as one of the founding fathers of artificial intel-ligence, Simon argued that economics was based on a faulty premise: individual rationality. From his perspective, people rarely made 'optimal' decisions as most economic theories assumed, but behaved according to simple rules of thumb that were not generally optimal but merely satisfac-tory. This idea of 'satisficing' behavior—a term Simon coined to provide a concrete alternative to the optimizing behaviour that is sacred to most mainstream economists—was greeted with hostility and disdain by the economics profession, which may have explained Simon's eventual shift from economics to computer science.

Despite these early critics, economics today is still dominated by a single paradigm of human behavior—a testament to the extraordinary achievements of one individual: Paul A. Samuelson. In 1947, Samuelson published his PhD thesis titled *Foundations of Economic Analysis*, which might have seemed presumptuous—especially coming from a doctoral candidate—were it not for the fact that it did, indeed, become the foun-dations of modern economic analysis (Samuelson 1947). In contrast to much of the economics literature at the time, which was often based on relatively informal discourse and diagrammatic exposition, Samuelson developed a formal mathematical framework for economic analysis that could be applied to a number of seemingly unrelated contexts. Samuelson's opening paragraph made his intention explicit (the italics are his):

> *The existence of analogies between central features of various theories implies the existence of a general theory which underlies the particular theories and unifies them with respect to those central features.* This fundamental principle of generalization by abstraction was enunciated by the eminent American mathematician E. H. Moore more than thirty years ago. It is the purpose of the pages that follow to work out its implications for theoretical and applied economics.

He then proceeded to lay the foundations for what is now known as microeconomics: the subject of the first graduate-level course in every economics PhD programme today. Along the way, Samuelson also made major contributions to welfare economics, general equilibrium theory, comparative static analysis and business-cycle theory, all in a single doctoral dissertation!

If there is a theme to Samuelson's thesis, it is the systematic application of scientific principles to economic analysis, much like the approach of modern physics. This was no coincidence. In Samuelson's fascinating account of the intellectual origins of his dissertation (Samuelson 1998), he acknowledged the following:

> Perhaps most relevant of all for the genesis of *Foundations*, Edwin Bidwell Wilson (1879–1964) was at Harvard. Wilson was the great Willard Gibbs's last (and, essentially only) protégé at Yale. He was a mathematician, a mathematical physicist, a mathematical statistician, a mathematical economist, a polymath who had done first-class work in many fields of the natural and social sciences. I was perhaps his only disciple.... I was vaccinated early to understand that economics and physics could share the same formal mathematical theorems (Euler's theorem on homogeneous functions, Weierstrass's theorems on constrained maxima, Jacobi determinant identities underlying Le Chatelier reactions, etc.), while still not resting on the same empirical foundations and certainties.

Much of the economics and finance literature since *Foundations* has followed Samuelson's lead in attempting to deduce implications from certain postulates such as utility maximization, the absence of arbitrage or the equalization of supply and demand. In fact, one of the most recent milestones in economics—rational expectations—is founded on a single postulate, around which a large and still-growing literature has developed.

In a recent article co-authored with physicist Mark Mueller (Lo and Mueller 2010), I have argued that this research programme is a reflection of a peculiar psychological disorder that seems to afflict economists exclusively: physics envy. We economists wish to explain 99% of all observable phenomena using three simple laws, like the physicists do, but we have to settle, instead, for ninety-nine laws that explain only 3%, which is terribly frustrating! However, several physicists have pointed out to me that if economists genuinely envied them, they would place much greater emphasis on empirical verification of theoretical predictions and show much less attachment to theories rejected by the data.[1] In fact, I believe we suffer from a much more serious affliction: theory envy.

The exalted role of theory in economics is not due to Samuelson alone, but was created by the cumulative efforts of a number of intellectual giants responsible for a renaissance in mathematical economics during the half century following the Second World War. One of these giants, Gerard Debreu (1991), provides an eyewitness account of this remarkably fertile period:

> Before the contemporary period of the past five decades, theoretical physics had been an inaccessible ideal toward which economic theory sometimes strove. During that period, this striving became a powerful stimulus in the mathematization of economic theory.

What Debreu is referring to is a series of breakthroughs that not only greatly expanded our understanding of economic theory, but also held out the tantalizing possibility of practical applications involving fiscal and monetary policy, financial stability and central planning. These breakthroughs included

- game theory (von Neumann and Morganstern, 1944; Nash, 1951),
- general equilibrium theory (Debreu, 1959),
- economics of uncertainty (Arrow, 1964),
- long-term economic growth theory (Solow, 1956),
- portfolio theory and capital-asset pricing (Markowitz, 1954; Sharpe, 1964; Tobin, 1958),
- option-pricing theory (Black and Scholes, 1973; Merton, 1973),
- macroeconometric models (Tinbergen, 1956; Klein, 1970),

---

[1] I am especially grateful to Doyne Farmer, Paul Mende and Mark Mueller for many illuminating discussions about the differences and similarities between physicists and economists.

- computable general equilibrium models (Scarf, 1973) and
- rational expectations (Muth, 1961; Lucas, 1972).

Many of these contributions have been recognized with the award of Nobel prizes, and they have permanently changed the field of economics from a branch of moral philosophy pursued by gentlemen scholars to a full-fledged scientific endeavour not unlike the deductive process with which Isaac Newton explained the motion of the planets from three simple laws. The mathematization of neoclassical economics is now largely complete, with dynamic stochastic general equilibrium models, rational expectations and sophisticated econometric techniques having replaced the less rigorous arguments of the previous generation of economists. But something is missing.

Even as Samuelson wrote his remarkable *Foundations*, he was well aware of the limitations of a purely deductive approach. In his introduction, he offered the following admonition.

> Only the smallest fraction of economic writings, theoretical and applied, has been concerned with the derivation of *operationally meaningful* theorems. In part at least this has been the result of the bad methodological preconceptions that economic laws deduced from *a priori* assumptions possessed rigor and validity independently of any empirical human behavior. But only a very few economists have gone so far as this. The majority would have been glad to enunciate meaningful theorems if any had occurred to them. In fact, the literature abounds with false generalization.
>
> We do not have to dig deep to find examples. Literally hundreds of learned papers have been written on the subject of utility. Take a little bad psychology, add a dash of bad philosophy and ethics, and liberal quantities of bad logic, and any economist can prove that the demand curve for a commodity is negatively inclined.

This surprisingly wise and prescient passage is as germane today as it was over half a century ago when it was first written, and all the more remarkable in that it was penned by a twenty-something-year-old graduate student. The combination of analytical rigour and practical relevance was to become a hallmark of Samuelson's research throughout his career, and despite his theoretical bent his command of industry practices and market dynamics was astonishing. Less gifted economists might have been able to employ similar mathematical tools and parrot his scientific demeanour, but few would be able to match Samuelson's ability to distil the economic essence of a problem and then solve it as elegantly and completely.

Unlike physics, in which pure mathematical logic can often yield useful insights and intuition about physical phenomena, Samuelson's caveat reminds us that a purely deductive approach may not always be appropriate for economic analysis. As impressive as the achievements of modern physics are, physical systems are inherently simpler and more stable than economic systems, hence deduction based on a few fundamental postulates is likely to be more successful in the former case than in the latter. Conservation laws, symmetry and the isotropic nature of space are powerful ideas in physics that do not have exact counterparts in economics because of the nature of economic interactions and the types of uncertainty involved.

And yet economics has become the envy of the other social sciences, in which there are apparently even fewer unifying principles and operationally meaningful theorems. Despite the well-known factions within economics, there is significant consensus among practising economists regarding the common framework of supply and demand, the principle of comparative advantage, the law of one price, income and substitution effects, net present value relations and the time value of money, externalities and the role of government, etc. While false generalizations certainly abound among academics of all persuasions, economics does contain many true generalizations as well, and these successes highlight important commonalities between economics and the other sciences.

Samuelson's genius was to be able to deduce operationally meaningful theorems despite the greater uncertainty of economic phenomena. In this respect, perhaps the differences between physics and economics are not fundamental, but are due, instead, to differences in degree along two dimensions: the amount of uncertainty and the role of empirical verification.

Although physics is no stranger to randomness—as the Heisenberg uncertainty principle and quantum mechanics attest—the vast majority of observable physical phenomena can nevertheless be explained by relatively simple deterministic relationships like 'force equals mass times acceleration' or 'attraction is inversely proportional to the square of the distance'. Moreover, such relationships have been in place and largely unchanged for the past 13.7 billion years. Economics knows no such simplicity or stability. Accordingly, controlled experimentation and empirical validation are possible in physics, and most theories can be conclusively affirmed or rejected, leading to a much closer collaboration between theorists and experimentalists. Not so in economics. Because our models are far less predictive—I believe 'stylized models' is the politically correct euphemism here—empirical research is often more an exercise in exploratory data analysis than a formal and definitive test of theory.

As a result, economic theories do not die easy deaths, but go in and out of fashion instead. Keynesian macroeconomics was the dominant theory in the aftermath of the Second World War among academics and policymakers, only to be discredited by the Lucas critique in the 1970s and replaced by rational expectations and stochastic dynamic general equilibrium models, which, in turn, have lost some credibility due to their failure to capture the recent financial crisis, paving the way for renewed interest in Keynes. No wonder Truman asked for a one-armed economist!

This cyclical nature of the history of economic thought suggests that cultural, political and historical circumstances may play a more influential role in economics than in the hard sciences, an inevitable consequence of the fact that human behaviour is at the centre of our discipline. As a result, economics can never rid itself of all imprecision and uncertainty. As the great physicist Richard Feynman put it, 'imagine how much harder physics would be if electrons had feelings'. However, until recently, mainstream economics had largely shunned the behavioural aspects of economic realities, preferring to focus instead on the orderly, antiseptic and internally consistent theories of expected utility maximization, rational expectations and efficient markets, even in the face of numerous well-documented and repeatable experimental and empirical violations. Theoretical foundations have become a hallmark of economics, making it unique among the social sciences, but any virtue can become a vice when taken to the extreme of theory envy. While economics has produced many genuine breakthroughs over the past half century, other fields have also developed unique insights about human behavior, and the intellectual gains from trade between these disciplines may be substantial.

This idea is embodied in the notion of 'consilience', a term reintroduced into the popular lexicon by E. O. Wilson (1998), who attributes its first use to William Whewell's 1840 treatise *The Philosophy of the Inductive Sciences*, in which Whewell wrote the following.

> The Consilience of Inductions takes place when an Induction, obtained from one class of facts, coincides with an Induction, obtained from another different class. This Consilience is a test of the truth of the Theory in which it occurs.

45

In comparing the rate of progress in the medical sciences versus the rate of progress in the social sciences, Wilson makes a sobering observation:

> There is also progress in the social sciences, but it is much slower, and not at all animated by the same information flow and optimistic spirit.
>
> The crucial difference between the two domains is consilience: the medical sciences have it and the social sciences do not. Medical scientists build upon a coherent foundation of molecular and cell biology. They pursue elements of health and illness all the way down to the level of biophysical chemistry.
>
> Social scientists by and large spurn the idea of the hierarchical ordering of knowledge that unites and drives the natural sciences. Split into independent cadres, they stress precision in words within their specialty but seldom speak the same technical language from one specialty to the next.

This is a bitter pill for economists to swallow, but it provides a clear directive for improving the status quo.

Rather than focusing solely on elegant theories, economics is at its Samuelsonian best when it marries rigorous theoretical and empirical analysis with practical challenges, using realistic assumptions regarding human cognitive abilities, institutional constraints and transaction costs. Economists need not shy away from sophisticated mathematics, but technique should be the servant, not the master, of a greater purpose. And when such analysis leads to a fork in research paths, one leading to elegant theory under counterfactual assumptions and the other to messier but more realistic empirical or experimental results, the latter should be given at least as much priority as the former. In this respect, economics may benefit from the examples of anthropology, psychology, the cognitive sciences and medicine, in which theories emerge inductively as well as deductively, motivated by empirical regularities and anomalies, and expeditiously discarded when they cannot explain the data.

This approach also has significant implications for how economics is taught. Unlike mathematics and physics, where gifted students can quickly develop intuition for some of the most fundamental concepts of the discipline, economics demands considerably greater institutional and historical context to achieve a comparable level of understanding. Although students of any introductory economics course can easily regurgitate the mathematics of supply and demand, until they witness the price-discovery process in action in a market that they care about, it is virtually impossible for them to fully appreciate both the power of the Marshallian cross as well as its many limitations in the face of trading costs, uncertainty, limited and asymmetric information, and institutional rigidities. As a result, the *enfant terrible* is almost unheard of in economics but commonplace in mathematics and the basic sciences.[2] One needs a minimum level of exposure to economic contexts and behaviour before being able to develop new insights into its inner workings.

One natural innovation is therefore to teach economics not from an axiomatic and technique-oriented perspective, but by posing challenges that can only be addressed through economic logic. Instead of starting microeconomics with the consumer's problem of maximizing utility subject to a budget constraint, begin by challenging students to predict the impact of a gasoline tax on the price of gasoline, or by asking them to explain why diamonds are so much more expensive than water despite the fact that the latter is critical for survival unlike the former. Instead of starting macroeconomics with national income accounts, begin with the question of how to measure and manage the wealth of nations, or by asking why inflation can be so disruptive to economic growth. Without the proper institutional, political and historical context in which to interpret economic models, constrained optimization methods and fixed-point existence proofs have much less meaning and are more likely to give rise to theory envy. However, when students understand the 'why' of their course of study, even the most complex mathematical tools can be mastered and are almost always applied more meaningfully.

For PhD students, gaining exposure to live economic environments before starting to write dissertations should be a priority, and can be accomplished via industry and government internships or field work. By observing or participating in real economic activity in the domain of their likely field of specialization, students will develop a much deeper sense of purpose as they begin their research careers in economics.

In my own case, this connection between theory and practice was the turning point for me during that fateful first semester in graduate school. I was saved by a single random conversation with a friend who suggested that I take a class at MIT taught by some professor named Merton. Such was my state of ignorance at the time that I had no idea what finance was about (balancing your chequebook?), much less who Robert Merton was or what his singular role was in developing the field I was about to choose for my career. Merton's lectures were unusually inspiring because of the remarkably close interplay between theory and practice in every topic he

---

[2]The precociousness of Paul Samuelson, discussed above, and Ronald Coase—whose seminal article 'The nature of the firm' was apparently based on his undergraduate thesis—is perhaps the exception that proves this rule.

tackled, to an extent I had never seen before in any other branch of the dismal science. Like all the other students who attended his lectures during those years, I now feel greatly privileged to have been an eyewitness during this formative period of modern financial economics.

With the benefit of hindsight and some practical experience, I now understand that because economic decisions often imply that there are winners and losers, public policy decisions will never be completely free of political considerations, nor should they be. But the demarcation between objective scientific analysis and the political considerations to which such analysis is just one of several inputs should be made as explicit as possible. When economists proffer dogmatic policy prescriptions motivated more by their own politics and arrogance than by scientific evidence, they undermine the credibility of the entire profession. The recent financial crisis has exposed some serious gaps in our understanding of the global economy, and the need to take stock and get our academic house in order has never been greater. This presents us with a precious opportunity to make wholesale changes to our discipline that would otherwise be impossible, so we should delay no longer. As Rahm Emanuel put it, 'Rule one: never allow a crisis to go to waste'.

REFERENCES

Debreu, G. 1991. The mathematization of economics. *American Economic Review* 81:1-7.

Lo, A., and M. Mueller. 2010. Warning: physics envy may be hazardous to your wealth. *Journal of Investment Management* 8:13-63.

Samuelson, P. 1947. *Foundations of Economic Analysis*. Cambridge, MA: Harvard University Press.

Samuelson, P. 1998. How *Foundations* came to be. *Journal of Economic Literature* 36:1375-1386.

Wilson, E. 1998. *Consilience*. New York: Alfred A. Knopf.

The Map Is Not the Territory:
An Essay on the State of Economics

By John Kay

The reputation of economics and economists, never high, has been a victim of the crash of 2008. The Queen was hardly alone in asking why no one had predicted it. An even more serious criticism is that the economic policy debate that followed seems only to replay the similar debate after 1929. The issue is budgetary austerity versus fiscal stimulus, and the positions of the protagonists are entirely predictable from their previous political allegiances.

The doyen of modern macroeconomics, Robert Lucas, responded to the Queen's question in a guest article in *The Economist* in August 2009 (Lucas 2009). The crisis was not predicted, he explained, because economic theory predicts that such events cannot be predicted. Faced with such a response, a wise sovereign will seek counsel elsewhere.

But not from the principal associates of Lucas, who are even less apologetic. Edward Prescott, like Lucas a Nobel laureate, began a recent address to a gathering of other laureates by announcing, 'this is a great time in aggregate economics'. Thomas Sargent, whose role in developing Lucas's ideas has been decisive, is more robust still (Sargent 2010). Sargent observes that criticisms such as Her Majesty's 'reflect either woeful ignorance or intentional disregard of what modern macroeconomics is about'. 'Off with his head', perhaps. But before dismissing such responses as ridiculous, consider why these economists thought them appropriate.

In his Nobel lecture in 1995 (Lucas 1995), Lucas described his seminal model. That model—now known as the dynamic stochastic general equilibrium model—developed into the dominant approach to macroeconomics today. In that paper, Lucas makes the following assumptions (among others): everyone lives for two periods, of equal length, working for one and spending in another; there is only one good, and no possibility of storage of that good or of investment; there is only one homogeneous kind of labour; there is no mechanism of family support between older and younger generations; and so on.

All science uses unrealistic simplifying assumptions. Physicists describe motion on frictionless plains and gravity in a world without air resistance, not because anyone believes that the world is frictionless and airless but because it is too difficult to study everything at once. A simplifying model eliminates confounding factors and focuses on a particular issue of interest. To put such models to practical use, you must be willing to bring back the excluded factors. You will probably find that this modification will be important for some problems and not others—air resistance makes a big difference to a falling feather but not to a falling cannonball.

But Lucas and those who follow him were plainly engaged in a very different exercise, as the philosopher Nancy Cartwright (2007) has explained. The distinguishing characteristic of their approach is that the list of unrealistic simplifying assumptions is extremely long. Lucas (1988) was explicit about his objective: 'the construction of a mechanical artificial world populated by interacting robots that economics typically studies'. An economic theory, he explains, is something that 'can be put on a computer and run'. Lucas has called structures like these 'analogue economies', because they are, in a sense, complete economic systems. They loosely resemble the world, but a world so pared down that everything about them is either known or can be made up. Such models are akin to Tolkien's Middle Earth, or a computer game like Grand Theft Auto.

The knowledge that every problem has an answer, even and perhaps especially if that answer is difficult to find, meets a deeply felt human need. For that reason, many people become obsessive about artificial worlds, such as computer games, in which they can see the connection between actions and outcomes. Many economists who pursue these approaches are similarly asocial. It is probably no accident that economics is by far the most male of the social sciences.

One might learn skills or acquire useful ideas through playing these games, and some users do. If the creators are good at their job, as of course they are, the sound effects, events and outcomes of a computer game resemble those we hear and see—they can, in a phrase that Lucas and his colleagues have popularized, be calibrated against the real world. But that correspondence does not, in any other sense, validate the model. The nature of such self-contained systems is that successful strategies are the product of the assumptions made by the authors. It obviously cannot be inferred that policies that work in Grand Theft Auto are appropriate policies for governments and businesses.

Yet this correspondence does seem to be what the proponents of this approach hope to achieve—and even claim they have achieved. The debate on austerity versus stimulus, in academic circles, is in large part a debate about the validity of a property called Ricardian equivalence, which is observed in this type of model. If government engages in fiscal stimulus by spending more or by reducing taxes, people will realize that such a policy means higher taxes or lower spending in future. Even if they seem to be better off today, they will be poorer in future, and by a similar amount. Anticipating this, they will cut back and government spending will crowd out private spending. Fiscal policy is therefore ineffective as a means of responding to economic dislocation.

In a more extended defence of the dynamic stochastic general equilibrium approach, John Cochrane, Lucas's University of Chicago colleague, puts forward the policy ineffectiveness thesis—immediately acknowledging that the assumptions that give rise to it 'are, as usual, obviously not true' (Cochrane 2009). For most people, that might seem to be the end of the matter. But it is not. Cochrane goes on to say that 'if you want to understand the effects of government spending, you have to specify why the assumptions leading to Ricardian equivalence are false'. That is a reasonable demand, though one that is easy to satisfy—as Cochrane himself readily acknowledges.

But Cochrane will not give up so easily. He goes on:

> Economists have spent a generation tossing and turning the Ricardian equivalence theory and assessing the likely effects of fiscal stimulus in its light, generalizing the 'ifs' and figuring out the likely 'therefores'. This is exactly the right way to do things.

The programme Cochrane describes modifies the core model in a rather mechanical way that makes it more complex, but not necessarily more realistic, by introducing additional parameters that have labels such as 'frictions' or 'transactions costs'—in much the same way as a game compiler might introduce a new module or sound effect.

Why is this 'exactly the right way to do things'? There are at least two alternative ways to proceed. You could build a different analogue economy. Joseph Stiglitz, for example, favours a model that retains many of Lucas's assumptions but gives critical importance to imperfections of information (Rothschild and Stiglitz 1976; Stiglitz 1977; Stiglitz and Weiss 1981). After all, Ricardian equivalence requires that households have a great deal of information about future budgetary options, or at least behave as if they did. A more radical modification might be an agent-based model, for example, which assumes that households respond routinely to events according to specific behavioural rules. Such models can also 'be put on a computer and run'. It is not obvious in advance—or, generally, in retrospect—whether the assumptions, or conclusions, of these models are more, or less, plausible than those of the kinds of model favoured by Lucas and Cochrane.

But another approach would discard altogether the idea that the economic world can be described by a universally applicable model in which all key relationships are predetermined. Economic behaviour is influenced by technologies and cultures, which evolve in ways that are certainly not random but which cannot be described fully, or perhaps at all, by the kinds of variables and equations with which economists are familiar. Models, when employed, must therefore be context specific, in the manner suggested in a recent book by Roman Frydman and Michael Goldberg (2007).

In that eclectic world, Ricardian equivalence is no more than a suggestive hypothesis. It is possible that some such effect exists. One might be sceptical about whether it is very large, and suspect that its size depends on a range of confounding and contingent factors: the nature of the stimulus, the overall political situation, the nature of financial markets and welfare systems. This is what the generation of economists who followed Keynes did when they estimated a consumption function—they tried to measure how much of a fiscal stimulus was spent—and the 'multiplier' that resulted.

But you would not nowadays be able to publish similar articles in a good economics journal. You would be told that your model was theoretically inadequate: it lacked rigour, failed to demonstrate consistency. You might be accused of the cardinal sin of being 'ad hoc'. Rigour and consistency are the two most powerful words in economics today.

They have undeniable virtues, but for economists they have particular interpretations. Consistency means that any statement about the world must be made in the light of a comprehensive descriptive theory of the world. Rigour means that the only valid claims are logical deductions from specified assumptions. Consistency is therefore an invitation to ideology, rigour an invitation to mathematics. This curious combination of ideology and mathematics is the hallmark of what is often called 'freshwater economics'—the name reflecting the proximity of Chicago, and other centres such as Minneapolis and Rochester, to the Great Lakes.

Consistency and rigour are features of a deductive approach, which draws conclusions from a group of axioms, and whose empirical relevance depends entirely on the universal validity of the axioms. The only descriptions that fully meet the requirements of consistency and rigour are complete artificial worlds, like those of Grand Theft Auto, which can 'be put on a computer and run'.

For many people, deductive reasoning is the mark of science, while induction, in which the argument is derived from the subject matter, is the characteristic method of history or literary criticism. But this is an artificial, exaggerated distinction. 'The first siren of beauty', says Cochrane, 'is logical consistency'. It seems impossible that anyone acquainted with great human achievements—whether in the arts, the humanities or the sciences—could really believe that the first siren of beauty is consistency. This is not how Shakespeare, Mozart or Picasso—or Newton or Darwin—approached their task.

The issue is therefore not mathematics versus poetry. Deductive reasoning of any kind necessarily draws on mathematics and formal logic; inductive reasoning is based on experience and above all on careful observation and may, or may not, make use of statistics and mathematics. Much scientific progress has been inductive: empirical regularities are observed in advance of any clear understanding of the mechanisms that give rise to them. This is true even of hard sciences such as physics, and more true of applied disciplines such as medicine or engineering. Economists who assert that the only valid prescriptions in economic policy are logical deductions from complete axiomatic systems take prescriptions from doctors who often know little more about these medicines than that they appear to treat the disease. Such physicians are unashamedly ad hoc; perhaps pragmatic is a better word. With exquisite irony, Lucas holds a chair named for John Dewey, the theorist of American pragmatism.

Engineers and doctors can perhaps be criticized for attaching too much weight to their own experience and personal observations. They are often sceptical, not just of theory, but of data they have not themselves collected. In contrast, most modern economists make no personal observations at all. Empirical work in economics, of which there is a great deal, predominantly consists of the statistical analysis of large data sets compiled by other people.

Few modern economists would, for example, monitor the behaviour of Procter & Gamble, assemble data on the market for steel or observe the behaviour of traders. The modern economist is the clinician with no patients, the engineer with no projects. And since these economists do not appear to engage with the issues that confront real businesses and actual households, the clients do not come.

There are, nevertheless, many well-paid jobs for economists outside academia. Not, any more, in industrial and commercial companies, which have mostly decided economists are of no use to them. Business economists work in financial institutions, which principally use them to entertain their clients at lunch or advertise their banks in fillers on CNBC. Economic consulting employs economists who write lobbying documents addressed to other economists in government or regulatory agencies.

The mutual disdain between economists and practical people is not a result of practical people not being interested in economic issues—many are obsessed with them. Frustrated, they base their macroeconomic views on rudimentary inductive reasoning, as in the attempts to find elementary patterns in data: will the recession be V-shaped, or L-shaped, or double dip? *Freakonomics* (Levitt and Dubner 2007), which applies simple analytic thinking to everyday problems, has been a best-seller for years. Elegantly labelled ideas that resonate with recent experience—the Minsky moment, the tipping point (Gladwell 2000), the Black Swan (Taleb 2007)—are enthusiastically absorbed into popular discourse.

If much of the modern research agenda of the economics profession is thus unconnected to the everyday world of business and finance, this is also largely true of what is taught to students. Most people finishing an undergraduate course today would not be equipped to read the *Financial Times*. They could import data on gross domestic product and consumer prices into a statistical package, and would have done so, but they would have no idea how these numbers were derived. They would be little better equipped than the average person in the street to answer questions such as, why are nationalized industries more efficient in France than in Britain? Why is a school teacher in Switzerland paid much more than an Indian one? Or the oldest of examination chestnuts, are cinema seats in London expensive because rents in London are high, or vice versa?

In a much-mocked defence of his recent graduate school education, Kartik Athreya (2010) explains—with approval—that

> much of my first year [PhD] homework involved writing down tedious
> definitions of internally consistent outcomes. Not analysing them, just
> defining them.

Many subjects involve tedious rote acquisition of essential basic knowledge (think law or medicine), but can it really be right that the essence of advanced economic training is checking definitions of consistency?

A review of economics education two decades ago concluded that students should be taught 'to think like economists'. But 'thinking like an economist' has come to be interpreted as the application of deductive reasoning based on a particular set of axioms. Another University of Chicago Nobel laureate, Gary Becker, offered the following definition: 'the combined assumptions of maximizing behavior, market equilibrium, and stable preferences, used relentlessly and consistently, form the heart of the economic approach' (Becker 1978). Becker's Nobel citation (Royal Swedish Academy of Sciences 1992) rewards him for 'having extended the domain of microeconomic analysis to a wide range of economic behavior'. But such extension is not an end in itself: its value can lie only in new insights into that behaviour.

'The economic approach' as described by Becker is not, in itself, absurd. What is absurd is the claim to exclusivity he makes for it: *a priori* deduction from a particular set of unrealistic simplifying assumptions is not just a tool but 'the heart of the economic approach'. A demand for universality is added to the requirements of consistency and rigour. Believing that economics is like they suppose physics to be—not necessarily correctly—economists like Becker regard a valid scientific theory as a representation of the truth: a description of the world that is independent of time, place, context or the observer. That is what Prescott has in mind in insisting on the term 'aggregate economics' instead of macroeconomics— there is, he explains, only economics.

The further demand for universality with the consistency assumption leads to the hypothesis of rational expectations and a range of arguments grouped under the rubric of 'the Lucas critique'. If there were to be such a universal model of the economic world, economic agents would have to behave as if they had knowledge of it, or at least as much knowledge of it as was available, otherwise their optimizing behaviour would be inconsistent with the predictions of the model. This is a *reductio ad absurdum* argument, which demonstrates the impossibility of any universal model: since the implications of the conclusion for everyday behaviour are preposterous, the assumption of model universality is false.

But this is not how the argument has been interpreted. Since the followers of this approach believe strongly in the premise—to deny that there is a single pre-specified model that determines the evolution of economic series would, as they see it, be to deny that there could be a science of economics—they accept the conclusion that expectations are formed by a process consistent with general knowledge of that model. It is by no means the first time that people blinded by faith or ideology have pursued false premises to absurd conclusions—and, like their religious and political predecessors, come to believe that those who disagree are driven by 'woeful ignorance or intentional disregard'.

This is not science, however, but its opposite. Properly conducted science is always provisional, and open to revision in the light of new data or experience. Much of modern macroeconomics, on the other hand, tortures data to demonstrate consistency with an *a priori* world view or elaborates the definition of rationality to render it consistent with any observed behaviour.

The fallacy here is well described by Donald Davidson (2000).

> It is perhaps natural to think there is a unique way of describing things which gets at their essential nature, 'an interpretation of the world which gets it right', as Rorty puts it, a description of 'Reality As It Is In Itself'. Of course, there is no such unique 'interpretation' or description, not even in the one or more languages each of us commands, not in any possible language. Or perhaps we should just say this is an idea of which no-one has made good sense.

And economists have not made good sense of it either, though they have been persistent in trying.

Economic models are no more, or less, than potentially illuminating abstractions. Another philosopher, Alfred Korzybski, puts the issue more briefly: 'the map is not the territory' (Korzybski 1931). Economics is not a technique in search of problems but a set of problems in need of solution. Such problems are varied and the solutions will inevitably be eclectic.

This is true for analysis of the financial market crisis of 2008. Lucas's assertion that 'no one could have predicted it' contains an important, though partial, insight. There can be no objective basis for a prediction of the kind 'Lehman Bros will go into liquidation on September 15', because if there were, people would act on that expectation and, most likely, Lehman would go into liquidation straight away. The economic world, far more than the physical world, is influenced by our beliefs about it.

Such thinking leads, as Lucas explains, directly to the efficient market hypothesis—available knowledge is already incorporated in the price of securities. And there is a substantial amount of truth in this—the growth prospects of Apple and Google and the problems of Greece and the Eurozone are all reflected in the prices of shares, bonds and currencies. The efficient market hypothesis is an illuminating idea, but it is not 'Reality As It Is In Itself'. Information is reflected in prices, but not necessarily accurately, or completely. There are wide differences in understanding and belief, and different perceptions of a future that can be at best dimly perceived.

In his *Economist* response, Lucas acknowledges that 'exceptions and anomalies' to the efficient market hypothesis have been discovered, 'but for the purposes of macroeconomic analyses and forecasts they are too small to matter'. But how could anyone know, in advance not just of this crisis but also of any future crisis, that exceptions and anomalies to the efficient market hypothesis are 'too small to matter'?

You can learn a great deal about deviations from the efficient market hypothesis, and the role they played in the recent financial crisis, from journalistic descriptions by people like Michael Lewis (2011) and Greg Zuckerman (2009), who describe the activities of some individuals who did predict it. The large volume of such material that has appeared suggests many avenues of understanding that might be explored. You could develop models in which some trading agents have incentives aligned with those of the investors who finance them and others do not. You might describe how prices are the product of a clash between competing narratives about the world. You might appreciate the natural human reactions that made it difficult to hold short positions when they returned losses quarter after quarter.

This pragmatic thinking, employing many tools, is a better means of understanding economic phenomena than Gary Becker's 'combined assumptions of maximizing behaviour, market equilibrium, and stable preferences, used relentlessly and consistently'—and to the exclusion of any other 'ad hoc' approach. More eclectic analysis would require not just deductive logic but also an understanding of processes of belief formation, anthropology, psychology and organizational behaviour, and meticulous observation of what people, businesses and governments actually do. You could learn nothing about how these things influence prices if you started with the proposition that deviations from a specific theory of price determination are 'too small to matter' because all that is knowable is already known and therefore 'in the price'. And that is why today's students do, in fact, learn nothing about these things, except perhaps from extracurricular reading.

What Lucas means when he asserts that deviations are 'too small to matter' is that attempts to construct general models of deviations from the efficient market hypothesis—by specifying mechanical trading rules or by writing equations to identify bubbles in asset prices—have not met with much success. But this is to miss the point: the expert billiard player plays a nearly perfect game (Friedman and Savage 1948), but it is the

57

imperfections of play between experts that determine the result. There is a (trivial) sense in which the deviations from efficient markets are too small to matter—and a more important sense in which these deviations are the principal thing that does matter.

The claim that most profit opportunities in business or in securities markets have been taken is justified. But it is the search for the profit opportunities that have not been taken that drives business forward— it is the belief that profit opportunities that have not been arbitraged away still exist that explains why there is so much trade in securities. Far from being 'too small to matter', these deviations from efficient market assumptions, not necessarily large, are the dynamic of the capitalist economy.

Such anomalies are idiosyncratic and cannot, by their very nature, be derived as logical deductions from an axiomatic system. The distinguishing characteristic of Henry Ford or Steve Jobs, Warren Buffett or George Soros is that their behaviour cannot be predicted from any pre-specified model. If the behaviour of these individuals could be predicted in this way, they would not have been either innovative or rich. But the consequences are plainly not 'too small to matter'.

The preposterous claim that deviations from market efficiency were not only irrelevant to the recent crisis but could never *be* relevant is the product of an environment in which deduction has driven out induction and ideology has taken over from observation. The belief that models are not just useful tools but are also capable of yielding comprehensive and universal descriptions of the world has blinded its proponents to realities that have been staring them in the face. That blindness was an element in our present crisis, and it conditions our still ineffectual responses. Economists—in government agencies as well as universities—were obsessively playing Grand Theft Auto while the world around them was falling apart.

REFERENCES

Athreya, K. 2010. Economics is hard: don't let bloggers tell you otherwise. Federal Bank of Richmond (17 June).

Becker, G. 1978. *The Economic Approach to Human Behavior.* University of Chicago Press.

Cartwright, N. 2007. *Hunting Causes and Using Them: Approaches in Philosophy and Economics.* Cambridge University Press.

Cochrane, J. H. 2009. How did Paul Krugman get it so wrong? Available at http://faculty.chicagobooth.edu/john.cochrane/research/papers/krugman_response.htm.

Davidson, D. 2000. *Rorty and His Critics.* Oxford: Blackwell.

Friedman, M., and L. J. Savage. 1948. The utility analysis of choices involving risk. *The Journal of Political Economy* 56(4):279–304.

Frydman, R., and M. Goldberg. 2007. *Imperfect Knowledge Economics: Exchange Rates and Risk.* Princeton University Press.

Gladwell, M. 2000. *The Tipping Point: How Little Things Can Make a Big Difference.* London: Little, Brown.

Korzybski, A. 1931. A non-Aristotelian system and its necessity for rigour in mathematics and physics. A paper presented before the American Mathematical Society at the New Orleans, Louisiana meeting of the American Association for the Advancement of Science (28 December). (Reprinted, 1994, in *Science and Sanity: An Introduction to Non-Aristotelian Systems and General Semantics.* Fort Worth, TX: Institute of General Semantics (first published 1933).)

Levitt, S. D., and S. J. Dubner. 2007. *Freakonomics.* Harmondsworth: Penguin.

Lewis, M. 2011. *The Big Short: Inside the Doomsday Machine* (reprint edition). New York: W. W. Norton.

Lucas, R. 1988. On the mechanics of economic development. *Journal of Monetary Economics* 22(1):3–42.

Lucas, R. 1995. Prize lecture. Available at www.nobelprize.org/nobel_prizes/economics/laureates/1995/lucas-lecture.html.

Lucas, R. 2009. In defence of the dismal science. *The Economist* 392(8643):67 (8 August).

Rothschild, M., and J. Stiglitz. 1976. Equilibrium in competitive insurance markets: an essay on the economics of imperfect information. *Quarterly Journal of Economics* 90(4):630–649.

Royal Swedish Academy of Sciences. 1992. Press Release (13 October 1992). Available at www.nobelprize.org/nobel_prizes/economics/laureates/1992/press.html.

Sargent, T. 2010. Interview with Thomas Sargent. *Region* 24(3):26–39 (September).

Stiglitz, J. 1977. Monopoly, non-linear pricing and imperfect information: the insurance market. *Review of Economic Studies* 44(3):407–430.

Stiglitz, J., and A. Weiss. 1981. Credit rationing in markets with imperfect information. *American Economic Review* 71(3):393–410.

Taleb, N. N. 2007. *The Black Swan: The Impact of the Highly Improbable.* London: Allen Lane.

Zuckerman, G. 2009. *The Greatest Trade Ever: The Behind-the-Scenes Story of How John Paulson Defied Wall Street and Made Financial History* (reprint edition). New York: Crown.

59

The Economy and Economic Theory in Crisis

By Alan Kirman

We are in a paradoxical situation. As a statistical physicist said to me recently, 'there could not be a more exciting time to study economics'. Yet students of economics confess to being bored and disappointed with what they are taught in their economics courses. Furthermore, a number of leading policymakers have said clearly that economic theory had been of no use to them in the crisis and have appealed for new approaches. The words of two such policymakers follow below.

> Macro models failed to predict the crisis and seemed incapable of explaining what was happening to the economy in a convincing manner. As a policymaker during the crisis, I found the available models of limited help. In fact, I would go further: in the face of the crisis, we felt abandoned by conventional tools. In the absence of clear guidance from existing analytical frameworks, policymakers had to place particular reliance on our experience. Judgement and experience inevitably played a key role.
>
> Jean-Claude Trichet, president of the ECB (2010)

> There is also a strong belief, which I share, that bad or, rather, over-simplistic and overconfident economics helped create the crisis. There was a dominant conventional wisdom that markets were always rational and self-equilibrating, that market completion by itself could ensure economic efficiency and stability, and that financial innovation and increased trading activity were therefore axiomatically beneficial.
>
> Adair Turner, chairman of the UK Financial Services Authority (2010)

At the same time, economists continue to explain that their models are more complete and more coherent than before and that we are, therefore, headed in the right direction. The confidence of macroeconomists before the crisis was epitomized by Lucas's observation that 'the central problem of depression-prevention has been solved'.[1]

---

[1] This quote is from Robert Lucas's 2003 presidential address to the American Economic Association.

But what is more troubling is that this confidence does not seem to have been undermined by the crisis. In this short paper I would like to give a brief historical account of how we wound up in this situation, provide some indicators of where we should be going, and finally make a few observations about how we teach economics and train economists.

THE HISTORY OF MACRO'S BLIND ALLEY

Since the end of the nineteenth century, economics has followed a path that has steadily led to its becoming more formal, more internally consistent and more detached from reality. From early on, some of the leading protagonists of economic theory, such as Walras, stated clearly that their aim was to develop a science, by which they meant something with the same status as physics, for example. What Walras had in mind was an internally consistent theory that could be expressed in mathematical terms. Yet, while economics was directly based on the model of classical mechanics, it moved in the middle of the twentieth century towards an axiomatic mathematical approach, whereas physics evolved differently. In Walras's time there was little to distinguish a 'mathematical' approach from a 'physical' one. Indeed Walras himself systematically referred to 'l'économie mathématique', mathematical economics, to distinguish himself from those whom he regarded as descriptive or institutional economists. As he observed with pride in a letter to Hermann Laurent (see Jaffe 1965), the mathematician:

> All these results are marvels of the simple application of the language of mathematics to the quantitative notion of need or utility. Refine this application as much as you will but you can be sure that the economic laws that result from it are just as rational, just as precise and just as incontrovertible as were the laws of astronomy at the end of the seventeenth century.

It is worth observing that at the beginning of the road leading to modern theoretical economics, although Walras (like many modern economists) was keen to claim mathematical respectability, mathematicians were far from convinced on many points. For example, Poincaré in his correspondence with Walras chided the latter for his assumptions of the 'infinite egoism' and 'infinite farsightedness' of economic agents. Unfortunately for economics, Poincaré's observations fell on deaf ears.

It was the wish to be scientific or mathematical that, I would argue, led economics further and further from being an empirically based science and more and more in the direction of an abstract, internally consistent but essentially unfalsifiable, theory. The first and most significant aspect of this evolution was the insistence on the notion of an essentially static equilibrium. This basic notion, which is at the heart of modern economics, was built explicitly on physics by Walras and the Lausanne School. Why, then, did it not evolve with physics rather than evolve towards pure mathematics? Mirowski (1989) explains that thermodynamics and the emphasis on entropy would suggest a system constantly moving towards disorder, which contradicted the Lausanne view.

Instead, economics took the path towards the axiomatic mathematical approach, in the Bourbaki tradition emphasized above all by Gerard Debreu. In what sense did this take us further from reality? Perhaps it is relevant to recall what Bourbaki[2] had to say on the subject.

> Why do applications [of mathematics] ever succeed? Why is a certain amount of logical reasoning occasionally helpful in practical life? Why have some of the most intricate theories in mathematics become an indispensable tool to the modern physicist, to the engineer, and to the manufacturer of atom-bombs? Fortunately for us, the mathematician does not feel called upon to answer such questions.
>
> Bourbaki (1949, *Journal of Symbolic Logic*)

Thus, in that spirit, the furthering of economic theory was seen as an avenue to more advanced models rather than a pursuit of explanations of economic phenomena. We economists thus became totally preoccupied by the properties of the economy in an equilibrium state. But, thanks to important results established in the 1970s, it became clear that, within our 'scientific' models, we had to abandon the concern with how equilibrium prices are established and how the economy evolves towards equilibrium (on general equilibrium results, see Sonnenschein (1972), Mantel (1974) and Debreu (1974)). Theorists have therefore concentrated on the properties, in particular the efficiency, of equilibrium states. They have insisted on the rigour of the analysis, not the realism of the assumptions.

In the end, the mathematical road we followed petered out in pure theory and has only remained as part of macroeconomic theory. The irony is that early pioneers of mathematical economics discussed economies in which individuals interacted, either through some price mechanism and market institutions, or directly with each other. Yet in modern macroeconomic models, individuals do not interact at all, but are instead subsumed into a representative individual. This avoids all the problems of

---

[2]Nicolas Bourbaki was, of course, a pseudonym for a group of mathematicians mainly based in Paris.

how an aggregate equilibrium is reached, and whether it would be unique. However, the idea that the economy behaves as a 'rational' individual is an assumption that is in no way theoretically justified.

If the only assumptions we want to make concern people's preferences and firms' technologies, it could not be shown that the economy would reach an equilibrium, nor that there was only one equilibrium. The answer to this weakness seemed to be simple: add assumptions about the way people interact and the institutions that govern them. Perversely, this was considered to be 'unscientific', while the assumption that the economy acts like an individual was not. Economists actually flaunted this perversion. Lucas, for example, explicitly rejected the idea of adding parameters to the basic model to allow for an adjustment process. In fact, he made it a 'principle' that one should not add anything to the basic assumptions when modelling the economy (Lucas 1980):

> Now, I am attracted to the view that it is useful, in a general way, to be hostile toward theorists bearing free parameters, so that I am sympathetic to the idea of simply capitalizing this opinion and calling it a Principle.

His 'Principle' made it impossible for economists following him to study out-of-equilibrium phenomena. Since, with the assumptions he considered scientific, we could show that an equilibrium exists, the economy should be studied in that state. Even if one introduces dynamics, the economy simply evolves through a sequence of equilibria, and thus business cycles are equilibrium phenomena. Hence, the implicit assumption was made that all markets clear instantaneously. In particular, recessions or depressions had to be attributed to some exogenous and unanticipated shock. But as Bertrand Russell (1998) said a long time ago:

> There are still many people in America who regard depressions as acts of God. I think Keynes proved that the responsibility for these occurrences does not rest with Providence.

Keynes 'proved' nothing of the sort, but he did give plausible arguments as to why depressions should be considered to be endogenous.

The behaviour of people and firms who satisfy axioms of 'rationality' given their preferences and technologies can be rigorously analysed, and formal conclusions can be drawn. However, those axioms are not based on careful observation of individuals' behaviour. Rather, as many great economists, from Pareto to Robbins to Hicks, have pointed out, they are based on introspection by economists! Thus we have limited ourselves to extremely restrictive assumptions on individual motivations and opportunities and put to one side the general problem of how the economy as a whole works.

Behavioural economists argue that, in any event, the empirically observed behaviour of individuals does not correspond to those standard axioms. They would argue, therefore, that it is not reasonable to construct more and more sophisticated models in which the behaviour of neither the individuals nor the aggregate matches that observed in reality.

The message here is clear: macroeconomists have intentionally locked themselves into a position that implies that they can only analyse crisis situations as if they were equilibria. And yet, in times of crisis we cannot be thought of as being 'in equilibrium', and, furthermore, crises are clearly the result of the endogenous dynamics of the system.

Note that this restrictive attitude is a rather recent development, and earlier macroeconomists were perfectly happy simply to assume relationships between aggregate variables. They used no more than a few allusions as to how people react in different situations to justify their macroeconomic relations and did not claim to have a mathematically consistent theory based on 'rational' individual behaviour.

I have argued up to this point that macroeconomists have, over the decades, painted themselves into such a tight corner thanks to this framework that they could not expect to analyse a major crisis. Yet, for many economists, the current crisis was largely financial rather than real and it was only *ex post* that the consequences were felt in the real economy. I would like to suggest that the theory underlying financial economics was also flawed—and has long been recognized to be so.

THE FLAWS OF FINANCIAL THEORY

The foundations of modern financial economics are usually traced back to the work of Bachelier, who developed the theoretical basis for the idea that the price of a financial asset must follow a random walk. Bachelier argued that the changes in the price of a financial asset should be random with mean zero; and by a limit argument for the sum of random variables he argued that the distribution of price changes should be Gaussian. This was the foundation for later developments such as Markowitz's optimal portfolio theory and for the Black–Scholes formula for pricing options. It can reasonably be regarded as the basis for the modern theory of finance. Indeed, the efficient markets hypothesis, which asserts that all relevant information on assets is contained in their market prices, is directly derived from Bachelier's ideas. It is, of course, at the heart of the arguments for letting financial markets operate without interference. But, just as was the case with general equilibrium theory and its underlying assumptions on individual rationality and on aggregation, there has been no shortage of warnings as to the validity of the theory.

Mandelbrot argued fiercely for many years against Bachelier's theory, pointing out a mass of empirical evidence contradicting its basic assumptions. He was one of the more recent critics from a long and distinguished line. Poincaré, in his report on Bachelier's thesis (cited in Courtault *et al.* (2002)), said that the assumption that underlay the thesis—that individuals act independently on their information—was manifestly false. As he pointed out, humans have a natural and unchanging tendency to herd. Therefore Bachelier's work could not accurately depict the evolution of the prices of financial assets. Keynes himself, along with mathematicians such as Levy and Kolmogorov, similarly pointed out the unreasonableness of Bachelier's assumptions (Keynes 1983).

Many economists have argued that there is a basic problem with the efficient markets hypothesis (see, for example, Shiller 2005). It argues that prices move because some new piece of information becomes available, leading to a revision of the expectations of market participants. But what is the empirical evidence for this? As Joulin *et al.* (2008) point out, if the efficient markets hypothesis is correct, the price should essentially be constant between two news items, moving suddenly around the release time of the news. The arrival of news should be the main determinant of price volatility. There are, however, various pieces of evidence suggesting that this picture is incorrect. Volatility is much too high to be explained only by changes in fundamentals. The volatility process itself is random, with highly non-trivial clustering and long-memory properties (for a collection of survey articles, see Teyssière and Kirman (2006)). As Joulin *et al.* explain, many of these properties look very similar to the endogenous noise generated by complex, non-linear systems with feedback, such as turbulent flows. Indeed it appears that most of the volatility arises from trading itself, through the very impact of trades on asset prices. This confirms the earlier results of Cutler *et al.* (1990). More recently, Bouchaud *et al.* (2004), using high-frequency data to decompose the volatility into a 'trade impact' component and a news component, reported that the former is dominant. Joulin *et al.* confirm this conclusion directly, comparing news events with price time series. Indeed, their main result is that most large jumps in prices are not related to any broadcast news, even if they extend the notion of 'news' to a collective market or sector jump. This array of evidence suggests that the mechanism governing the formation of prices in financial markets is much more subtle than that contained in most standard equilibrium models.

ALTERNATIVE APPROACHES

From everything that I have said it should be clear that economics is unlikely to find its salvation by modifying its standard macro and financial models to deal with the difficulties they face. Yet the general sentiment within the profession has been precisely that economics has been making steady progress over recent years by incorporating various 'imperfections' into its models. A particular example of this is the plethora of models dealing with asymmetric information. But the more fundamental questions—of whether we should adhere to our equilibrium notions, using perfect competition as our benchmark model, and continue to base our analysis on rational individuals—still remain to be answered.

The answer needs to start with making direct interaction a central feature of aggregate models. This means abandoning the isolated *homo economicus* and thinking instead of an economy made up of individuals, firms and other collectivities that follow simple rules of behaviour but are affected by their neighbours. We may not always need to know how individuals take their decisions and in many cases we could be content with statistical aggregates. Many economists would see this approach as a violation of a golden rule in terms of assumptions, but the sort of system I am describing may have much better-defined dynamics than those mooted for standard economic models. This is not surprising since the standard models are not dynamic in any meaningful sense.

If we do wish to adhere to an equilibrium approach, it should not reflect convergence to a stationary state but perhaps instead to a limit distribution of states (see Foellmer *et al.* 2005). We could then model the dynamics of the economy as a sequence of temporary equilibria or, better, we could model the out-of-equilibrium dynamics directly, rather than having the only dynamics stem from periodic exogenous shocks. Large-scale interactive systems have been studied in great detail in other disciplines such as statistical physics, and we should take advantage of that analysis in economics.

Again, we should heed the lessons of behavioural economics and no longer attribute such remarkably implausible omniscience to the agents we model. Agents may not be 'irrational' in the sense that they act against their own interests but they surely do not exhibit the sort of intertemporal

67

consistency in their decisions that we attribute to them. They certainly do not have 'rational expectations'. As Bernanke said:[3]

> I just think it is not realistic to think that human beings can fully antic- ipate all possible interactions and complex developments. The best approach for dealing with this uncertainty is to make sure that the system is fundamentally resilient and that we have as many fail-safes and back-up arrangements as possible.

We must devote much more time to examining and analysing empiri- cal data on individuals' behaviour. We could then move away from the assumptions we typically make on the basis of introspection and replace them with assumptions based on regularities in observed behaviour.

Finally, if we are to accept that direct interactions between individuals are an essential feature of the economy, then we have to study the impact of the structure of that interaction. This means modelling the network of links between the individuals and institutions, specifying the nature of the nodes and links and, in addition, establishing criteria for determining their robustness. Here, however, there is an interesting problem with the economist's approach to networks. Economists wish to develop a very general theory and, in particular, one which is based on individual maxi- mizing behaviour. As Goyal (2007) describes it:

> The distinctiveness of the economic approach lies in the different methodology that is used.... These differences can be traced to a sub- stantive methodological premise in economics: social and economic phenomena must ultimately be explained in terms of the choices made by rational agents.

This quotation reveals two things: both the economist's quest for a very general abstract model encompassing many of the empirical phe- nomena that we observe, and also the wish to model using the basis of the same micro-foundations discussed earlier that have been shown to be inadequate. In fact, if, as I and others have claimed (Haldane and May 2011), we have to consider networks as an integral feature of the econ- omy, viewed as a complex adaptive system, we need a very different basis for our models.

A striking example of the value of starting from empirical data to estab- lish the nature of a network is provided by Vitali *et al.* (2011). They use a large database of the shareholdings of firms to establish the nature of the

---

[3]The quote comes from a 2010 interview with the *International Herald Tribune* (17 May).

network of ownership. Their findings, which have provoked considerable discussion, are remarkable:

> Nearly 4/10 of the control over the economic value of TNCs [trans-national corporations] in the world is held, via a complicated web of ownership relations, by a group of 147 TNCs in the core, which has almost full control over itself.

Unsurprisingly, three-quarters of these companies are banks.

An important point is that there is no evidence that this structure was intentional. There was no giant conspiracy—rather, the network evolved endogenously in this way. However, concentrated power in the hands of a few has clear implications for global financial stability, as recent events have shown. Starting from the empirical evidence, the authors were able to build a picture of the structure of the network and then to empha-size the implications of that structure for the stability of the network. Building on the their approach could potentially help policymakers and economists to find ways to stabilize financial markets.

There are new tools that could be used. Econophysics, though proba-bly too preoccupied with finding structure in financial time series, has a number of useful tools that we can use. A very good example is provided by Gabaix (2011). He explains how the shocks that cause major macro-economic turnarounds can arise from shocks to individual firms. As he says, since modern economies are dominated by large firms, idiosyn-cratic shocks to these firms can lead to non-trivial aggregate shocks. For instance, he explains that in the Republic of Korea the top two firms (Sam-sung and Hyundai) together account for 35% of exports, and the sales of those two firms account for 22% of Korean gross domestic product. In Japan, the top ten firms account for 35% of exports. With a realistic specifi-cation of the distribution of firm sizes, we no longer need to look for artifi-cial explanations for macroeconomic shocks. The basic idea is taken from modern physics, where power laws and fat-tailed distributions are com-mon currency. Although this approach contravenes the usual assumption of large numbers of firms facing shocks that are independent and thus in the aggregate negligible, it was nevertheless published in one of the lead-ing journals in economics, *Econometrica*. The profession has therefore clearly not been unaware of this sort of approach. Still, it has, in macro-economics at least, regarded it as marginal. Yet when Gabaix's arguments are coupled with those of Vitali *et al.*, we are immediately led to a view of the evolution of the economy that looks very different from the standard macroeconomic models.

There are many other approaches that will help us to develop new ways of looking at the economy. Although we will never develop a complete understanding of how our decision processes work, neuroeconomics points up some interesting features of our behaviour. Experimental economics has been very useful in showing up behavioural anomalies. Experiments in economics have been tied into a very restrictive framework to make them 'scientifically respectable', but they still have a role to play in showing that people do not behave as we assume them to. And now 'field experiments' have appeared on the scene and seem to offer a more realistic if less controllable way of analysing decisions. There is now such a wealth of data available that it is no longer possible to argue that we cannot observe people's behaviour in detail.

TRAINING ECONOMISTS

Here is the biggest problem of all. Nobody would contest the fact that the phenomena that economics claims to analyse are of enormous importance. Economics is surely, at least potentially, the most exciting discipline there is. And yet, if we proceed, as we usually do, by arguing that students have to master the 'basics', we are immediately faced with two problems: firstly, the students do not understand what relevance this has to the real-world problems that interested them in economics in the first place; and secondly, they find the approach extremely boring. But if we believe that economics can only turn over a new leaf through the work of a new generation of young economists, where are these to come from? How are we to generate the same enthusiasm among our students that we find in students of evolutionary or molecular biology, or astrophysics?

One answer, and a somewhat radical one, would be to argue that we should no longer begin our economics courses by examining the rational agent and his behaviour and then model him within the benchmark model of perfect competition. We could start with the basis of another paradigm, one in which externalities and the impact of one agent's behaviour on another are central to the model and in which agents continually bump into each other, and not only in market contexts (I recommend this approach in Kirman (2010)). While this would certainly bring a breath of fresh air and excitement to the subject, the student who learned only along these lines would have no idea of what economics is currently about. Would we be doing them a favour? As Max Planck once remarked, 'Physics is not about discovering the true laws which govern the universe, it is what physicists do'. In just the same way economics is what economists do and students should be able to read the papers in the field, if not in *Econometrica* at least in the *American Economic Review*.

There is a myth that economics is marked by steady progress towards the truth and a consequent reluctance to abandon any of the routes that we have pursued in recent years. But reading Walras, Pareto, Jevons, Marshall, Robbins and Hicks, to name but a few, we see how much we have also lost in our relentless pursuit of increasingly technical models with increasingly restrictive assumptions that are less and less related to reality.

As Bob Solow (2007) said:

> Maybe there is in human nature a deep-seated perverse pleasure in adopting and defending a wholly counterintuitive doctrine that leaves the uninitiated peasant wondering what planet he or she is on.

But we have to teach differently if we are to get our students engaged. The present challenge is to teach standard economic theory but with clear indications as to where its difficulties and inconsistencies lie. It is therefore extremely helpful to follow a course in the history of economic theory. It teaches that our discipline is highly path dependent, and that some of the choices made in the past have contributed to making the subject stagnate rather than advance.

At least three other productive routes are available.

Firstly, experimental economics is very useful to illustrate standard theory and much more enjoyable than a purely theoretical course (for an excellent example, see Bergstrom and Miller (1999)). It is also useful as an antidote to the standard assumptions on rationality, particularly in examining how people actually make decisions in situations with uncertainty.

Secondly, behavioural economics reinforces this by revealing how important psychological considerations are in determining people's choices and behaviour.

Thirdly, it is essential that the student gets his or her hands dirty early on by actually collecting and analysing data about some empirical phenomenon of his or her choice. When invited to do this in courses I have taught, students have collected price data from the local market and have tried to explain the location of low-income housing, the price of petrol on motorways, or the relative crime rates in two cities. Their aim was to explain some phenomenon they had observed and to see to what extent the economics that they had learned helped them in this. This simple

71

exercise changed their attitude and made them much more positive about economics.

Perhaps we should also rethink the nature of some of our courses. One obvious idea would be to teach a course on markets. The notion of a 'market economy' is invoked from the outset in economics course, but what markets are, how they operate and how they have evolved is hardly mentioned. It would be easy and informative to teach a course in which one would survey the role of markets in history, their different institutions and how they function for different commodities. The student would also find out, for example, how the stock exchange works and how prices are formed there, how the order book works and so forth. Such a course would have a historical and comparative component but would also offer a good background for theoretical work on perfect and imperfect competition. It would set out the difference between markets organized on an auction basis, those where prices are negotiated and those where prices are posted. Of course, this cuts right across the standard segmentation of our field but that is probably just how it should be.

What the student would learn in this context might be somewhat disconcerting, because he would find out that Walras, although he talked about the stock exchange, had little idea about how it actually functioned, while Marshall's account of the corn market suggests that he never set foot in one. The student would therefore realize that the disconcerting lack of interest in how the economy actually works is longstanding and not just a byproduct of the recent formalization of economics!

Although the market economy and market equilibrium are considered to be central features of our theory, markets as structures play almost no role in economics, which is one reason the subject can seem so abstract and unrealistic. As North (1977) said:

> It is a peculiar fact that the literature on economics…contains so little discussion of the central institution that underlies neoclassical economics—the market.

North's major contribution to economic thought was to insist that market institutions are indeed important (see North 1990). To an anthropologist, such an assertion seems trivial (see, for example, the remarkable work on the functioning of the Moroccan bazaar by Geertz *et al.* (1979)). But not so, for the theoretical economist. North is at pains to explain that closer analysis of institutions is essential to economic history, yet economic theory tends to focus on timeless and frictionless transactions. He therefore suggests that institutional analysis is an appropriate way of using some of the lessons from neoclassical economic theory in economic history, but he does not go on to suggest that theory itself might need to be substantially modified in the light of the institutional considerations that he raises in his historical research.

However, a more radical position is that, if we are to take markets seriously as places, whether virtual or geographical, where individuals interact directly and influence each other, then economic theory itself has to be modified. Rather than simply look at the constraints imposed by institutions and apply standard theory within those constraints, it would be better to develop a theory encompassing the emergence of those constraints. Markets are complicated phenomena; even for the same product they are far from uniform in their structure. Their rules change and they are restricted more or less strongly by government regulation. They self-organize and evolve over time. Given their importance in the economy, it seems unreasonable to leave their organization and evolution to one side.

One last remark is in order on this subject. If we do discuss markets at all, we typically do so by describing their role in achieving an efficient allocation of resources. When they do not do this we talk about 'market failure'. The basic idea is that markets are machines or mechanisms that process the available information and make it available. But in fact markets are composed of individuals. These individuals are learning, and, furthermore, market institutions evolve over time. When talking about the double problem posed firstly by the level of the national debt of certain countries and secondly by the amount of that debt held by various large banks, George Soros remarked recently that 'markets simply do not have the experience to handle this sort of problem'.[4] This is particularly enlightening because it raises the question of just how consistent the collective opinions revealed by the markets are. If they were the infallible information-processing machines that Hayek had in mind (Hayek 1945), Soros's observation would make no sense. However, if the collective opinion revealed by market prices is rather volatile and markets are thought of as 'learning', then the idea is consistent with what Soros seems to have in mind.

In such situations, how are policymakers supposed to know what markets 'want'? The obvious answer would be to find out by trial and error. This could be very costly and, if market opinion is volatile and transient, the lessons to be learned from the implications of their reactions to policy

---

[4]Soros interview with *Le Monde* (November 2011).

measures are far from clear. We are victims of the idea that the market 'has an opinion' but it is not at all obvious that this is a meaningful idea, because the prices supposed to indicate that opinion are the result of transactions between two people with different views. Thus, at best, when observing a movement in one direction one can argue that there is more weight on one side of the market than on the other. But a negative reaction to a particular policy measure may mean that some individuals think that the action taken was not severe enough or that it was so severe that it will have undesirable consequences. This is precisely the problem with the current austerity measures and their effect on growth. Thus, the idea that markets are simply vehicles for transmitting information is one we have to revise.

Perhaps the most important lesson one should convey in teaching economics is that the economy is a messy system that is far from being optimal and that people behave in a very 'noisy' manner. Nevertheless, these noisy individuals self-organize and manage to coordinate and achieve a great deal. Sometimes we look at social insects to see how, with very limited and local knowledge, they manage to sustain the life of the colony and to construct elaborate structures. Well-trained economists are happy to use evolutionary explanations of how these colonies have adapted optimally to their environment. They use this as an analogy to explain how people, without actually consciously doing so, similarly learn to optimize. But those who find this comforting should take the advice of Deborah Gordon, the well-known entomologist: 'watch the ants'. As she points out, after several weeks of watching ants at work, the observer wants nothing more than to help them, since they are doing such a poor job. Nevertheless, the nest is built, the Queen is fed and the colony survives despite predators and sudden changes in the environment. Our students should watch people making choices and pursuing their economic activities. When a supplier disappears, someone else takes his place, albeit not necessarily doing exactly the same thing. How all of this is coordinated is perhaps the most fascinating aspect of economics. The simple act of observing economic activity concentrates the mind wonderfully.

CONCLUSION

Our basic paradigm in economics is recognized as being extremely deficient. We have to develop economic theory that allows us to incorporate some of the lessons we have learned, including from our incapacity to analyse the sudden unanticipated large movements that have hit our economies. Describing these as due to some exogenous shocks that we cannot identify is to abdicate our responsibilities as economists.

A new vision should be one based on a system of interacting agents and institutions, one that is not in equilibrium in the conventional sense and one that will periodically go through major and sudden changes. It is probably wrong to hope for a general and comprehensive model such as that which was envisaged by general equilibrium theorists. We may have to learn from statistical physics and other disciplines and accept that there is a great deal of path dependence in the system, which implies that there will be no universal recipes for particular problems. However, this may lead us to a more pragmatic approach to economic policymaking.

Lastly, we should accept that the world is very 'noisy' and that the individuals within it act stochastically, not against their own interests but with a very limited view of what those interests are and with an even vaguer understanding of the impact individual actions have on the system. In such a world, contagion, panic, optimism and pessimism are key features and not just annoying imperfections.

We will have to keep teaching students economics as currently envisioned by economists, but this should not prevent us from opening students' eyes to the difficulties and challenges our discipline faces. This, in turn, may make them much more enthusiastic about understanding economic phenomena and trying to analyse them, rather than boring them with what they see as interminable and irrelevant technicalities.

REFERENCES

Bergstrom, T., and J. Miller. 1999. *Experiments with Economic Principles: Microeconomics.* McGraw-Hill.

Bouchaud, J.-P., Y. Gefen, M. Potters and M. Wyart. 2004. Fluctuations and response in financial markets: the subtle nature of 'random' price changes. *Quantitative Finance* 4:176–190.

Courtault, J.-M., Y. Kabanov, B. Bru, P. Crepel, I. Lebon and A. Le Marchand. 2002. Louis Bachelier on the centenary of *Théorie de la Spéculation.* In *Louis Bachelier: Aux Origines de la Finance Mathématique* (ed. J. M Courtault and Y. Kabanov). Paris: Universitaires Franc-Comtoises.

Cutler, D. M., J. M. Poterba and L. H. Summers. 1990. Speculative dynamics and the role of feedback traders. *American Economic Review* 80(2):63–68.

Debreu, G. 1974. Excess demand functions. *Journal of Mathematical Economics* 1:15–23.

Foellmer, H., U. Horst and A. Kirman. 2005. Equilibria in financial markets with heterogeneous agents: a probabilistic perspective. *Journal of Mathematical Economics* 41:123–155.

Gabaix, X. 2011. The granular origins of aggregate fluctuations. *Econometrica* 79:733–772.

Geertz, C., H. Geertz and L. Rosen. 1979. *Meaning and Order in Moroccan Society: Three Essays in Cultural Analysis.* Cambridge University Press.

Goyal, S. 2007. *Connections: An Introduction to the Economics of Networks.* Princeton University Press.

Haldane, A., and R. May. 2011. Systemic risk in banking ecosystems. *Nature* 469: 351–355.

Hayek, F. A. 1945. The use of knowledge in society. *American Economic Review* 35(4):519–530.

Jaffe, W. 1965. *Correspondence of Léon Walras,* letter number 1454. Elsevier.

Joulin, A., A. Lefevre, D. Grunberg and J.-P. Bouchaud. 2008. Stock price jumps: news and volume play a minor role. Preprint (arXiv:0803.1769).

Keynes, J. M. 1983. Review of Louis Bachelier's *Calcul des Probabilités.* In *Collected Articles of John Maynard Keynes.* Macmillan/Cambridge University Press.

Kirman, A. 2010. *Complex Economics: Individual and Collective Rationality.* Abingdon: Routledge.

Lucas, R. 1980. Methods and problems in business cycle theory. *Journal of Money Credit and Banking* 12(4):696–715.

Mantel, R. 1974. On the characterisation of aggregate excess demand. *Journal of Economic Theory* 7:348–353.

Mirowski, P. 1989. *More Heat than Light: Economics as Social Physics, Physics as Nature's Economics.* Cambridge University Press.

North, D. 1977. Markets and other allocation systems in history. *Journal of European Economic History* 6:703–716.

North, D. 1990. *Institutions, Institutional Change and Economic Performance.* Cambridge University Press.

Russell, B. 1998. *Autobiography,* 2nd edn, chapter 3, p. 69. Abingdon: Routledge.

Shiller, R. 2005. *Irrational Exuberance,* 2nd edn. Princeton University Press.

Solow, R. 2007. Reflections on the survey. In *The Making of an Economist, Redux* (ed. D. Colander). Princeton University Press.

Sonnenschein, H. 1972. Market excess demand functions. *Econometrica* 40:549–563.

Teyssière, G., and A. Kirman (eds). 2006. *Long Memory in Economics.* Springer.

Vitali, S., J. B. Glattfelder and S. Battiston. 2011. The network of global corporate control. *PLoS ONE* 6(10):e25995.

Experience Matters in the Education of Economists

By Edward Glaeser

The great challenge in educating economists is the wide range of roles played by dismal scientists. Current PhD programmes are meant to train scholars who can produce professional economics research that will be published in peer-reviewed journals. Generally they succeed in that worthy task.

Yet the world often expects economists to be able to contribute constructively to significant debates over economic policy, and making useful practical contributions requires a totally different set of skills to the ones needed for writing economics papers. But while one could imagine retooling PhD programmes to be more policy relevant, I suspect that would be a mistake. I am not sure that PhD programmes can even do a good job of delivering the wisdom, insight and institutional knowledge that represent the bare minimum needed for sound economic policymaking.

I teach the first segment of microeconomic theory taught to PhD students at Harvard, and I begin the course by telling our students that they have now, perhaps unwittingly, entered a trade school. Undergraduate economics typically tries to create broadly educated young people who can thoughtfully assess the world around them. Graduate education is meant to teach a craft: the ability to produce publishable articles that teach the world something about itself.

The students have every incentive to learn this craft. Their first job will largely depend on their 'job market' paper. Their chances for tenure will largely depend on the portfolio of papers they produce in their first five or six years of teaching. They will not travel far along the academic path without the ability to produce cutting-edge empirical work or theoretical papers that are either clever or deep.

The trade-school orientation of PhD programmes leads to two questions. Are we teaching this research task tolerably well? Should economics PhD programmes aim overwhelmingly to train students to produce the contemporary style of economic research?

The current mix of skills taught by PhD programmes includes understanding, and hopefully creating, formal economic theory, statistically testing hypotheses, with a heavy emphasis on causal inference, and managing the tricky marriage of theory and data. Students are exposed to field-specific literatures, which teach them what is known and what mature scholars would like to know. Perhaps, most importantly, students spend years writing and presenting research papers. There is no substitute for learning-by-doing.

Somewhat oddly, economics has recently moved towards less, rather than more, specialization, which is quite odd given Adam Smith's insights on the division of labour. While there was a clear line between theorists and empiricists in the 1970s and 1980s, the decreasing cost of doing empirical work means that there are now more generalists. PhD programmes certainly try to ensure that students have some ability to work with both theory and data.

Do our programmes teach the wrong mix of skills for producing professional researchers and paper writers? Like everyone who teaches PhD students, I have my own set of prejudices about where the current system falls short. I believe that faculty members tend to overemphasize their own research passions and under-inform students about the risks of particular research topics. Like most microeconomists, I think that first-year sequences spend too much time on macroeconomics, which seems—for historical reasons—to enjoy an extraordinarily privileged pedagogical place, given that it is only one field among many.

Yet these personal complaints are minor quibbles. Overall, PhD programmes do a good job of training students to write peer-reviewed papers. The heavy competition across these programmes helps to ensure that they teach to that key task. Indeed, the remarkable speed with which PhD programmes have brought psychological realism into the mainstream is a testament to their openness and to the widespread hunger for intellectual breakthroughs.

The complaints that are voiced about economics PhD programmes are more typically related to the second question. The critics often question the social returns to writing peer-reviewed papers. They often argue that economists, trained to write for *Econometrica*, seem to have learned little that is actually useful in practical policymaking.

On one level, these critics are right. It is certainly unclear that wise policymaking needs a broad knowledge of game-theoretic equilibrium refinements or simulated method-of-moments estimators. Modern economics training does not deliver worldly philosophers who can sit down with a Treasury Secretary and sagely discuss the promise and pitfalls of pressing policy options.

Many proposals about improving economics education reflect a desire to produce more well-rounded young scholars who can connect more meaningfully with the larger world. Economic history and history of thought provide the historical perspective that is a vital component of policy wisdom. Institutional knowledge is critical for anyone seeking to contribute to meaningful policy debate. But while reading Schumpeter or Ricardo is always enlightening about deep, lasting questions, it is not obviously of much practical use to the younger scholar whose passion is running randomized experiments in sub-Saharan Africa. I do not think, though, that economics PhD programmes should be reoriented from the writing of research papers to a quest for worldly wisdom.

I will happily claim that the research and paper-writing crafts, taken as a whole, create enormous social value. Many papers, perhaps even the majority of those that are published, may do relatively little for the world. But papers are options. The less-informative ones are forgotten and the good ones change history. Deep research, published in the most esoteric of journals, has ultimately had a significant impact on policy areas from monetary policy to auction design. It is entirely possible that the welfare benefits brought from economic theory to the spectrum auction alone completely covered the total costs of National Science Foundation spending on economics for at least a decade.

Moreover, core economic research has entered a period of high policy relevance. Cutting-edge work using randomization is remaking the world of aid to developing countries and education in the developed world. Researchers like Abhijit Banerjee, Esther Duflo and Michael Kremer are training students whose work profoundly informs the critical tasks for countries moving from poverty to prosperity. There may be less of the heroic theory that was written in the immediate post-war epoch, but the empirical work of young economists today is more valuable than ever.

Worldly wisdom is anyway best acquired over years of experience and searching for truth, not in a short sharp shock of intensive education, like that delivered in a PhD programme. In a few semesters of hard coursework, it is quite possible to learn the basics of econometric theory or mechanism design. The Ivory Tower is not the place to understand the many things that can go wrong with any policy innovation.

The current system, more or less, involves training young scholars to write papers, pushing them to write pure research for a decade or so until they get tenure, and then letting them choose whether to stick with writing papers or to follow some more applied occupation, like providing policy advice. This system allows wisdom to accrete over time and does not require PhD programmes to take on a wider mission.

While economics has many failings, the core system is not broken. We have not fully understood massive events, like the recent recession, and we certainly lack a consensus on how to respond to the downturn. Yet these failings do not reflect a lack of policy-relevant knowledge or a lack of history of thought or the study of institutions. The understanding of macroeconomics will always be limited by the lack of randomized trials and repetition.

If policymakers are concerned with ensuring that economic research is more focused on policy-relevant topics and ensuring that there are more policy-relevant economists, then research funding provides the most natural tool for reform. The Bank of England, or the Federal Reserve System, has every right to fund only research on applied research topics that are close to their core mission. As funds flow more freely to policy-related topics, more economists will work on those topics and more graduate students will be pulled into those areas.

Moreover, policymaking institutions concerned about a dearth of worldly philosophers could do more to entice young, probably recently tenured, economists from paper writing to policy relevance. They could offer more fellowships to visit and interact with public institutions. They could create more venues in which economists are rewarded for interacting with policymakers. I am not sure that this is a better use of economists' time than writing peer-reviewed papers, but institutions that want more policy-relevant economists can certainly try to make that happen.

While I do not think that PhD programmes are the natural place to inculcate policy relevance, there may be more that can be done to teach policy-relevant economics to undergraduates. Undergraduates do want to understand public policy. They do not need the wisdom to advise policymakers, but only the sense to make reasonable decisions about ordinary political actions, like voting. That is a lower and more reachable hurdle. The natural way of influencing undergraduate curricula is to provide financial support for undergraduate teaching.

I believe in the breadth of knowledge that comes with history of economic thought and institutional knowledge. I think that it is impossible to have real policy-relevant insight without knowing one's history and details about the real world. But not every economist needs to deliver policy-relevant insight—good, solid research that teaches the world about itself is a sufficient contribution. We should trust PhD programmes to deliver competent researchers and hope that later experience provides the judgement that the wider world demands.

The Education of Economists in the Light of the Financial Crisis

By Paul Seabright

In this short chapter I want to ask whether the continuing financial and economic crisis has taught us anything useful about how the education of undergraduate and postgraduate economists could be improved, and also whether the crisis has made it more likely that the necessary changes will in fact come about. The outlook for such changes is not promising. In the aftermath of the Great Depression there were important changes in the way economics was both studied and taught, but today's conditions, both in North America and in Europe, are very different. Most importantly, the Roosevelt administration vastly increased the numbers of economists employed by the federal government (similar changes occurred in Europe but on a smaller scale). While some degree of idealism and reaction to the events of the 1930s undoubtedly played a part in shaping what was taught, the expansion of job opportunities also created an incentive to create and remodel university courses to meet this demand; ideas and incentives complemented one another.

Today there are no such equivalent incentives. There are severe financial pressures on universities everywhere (which will be strongest for publicly funded universities because of fiscal constraints). These will tempt economics departments to fall back on easily evaluated teaching methods at the expense of those that may yield greater relevance but are harder to assess with simple evaluation techniques. Courses will be tailored to an even greater degree to meet the demand of private-sector employers, even though it was precisely the fact that the incentives of private-sector firms did not reflect the wider interests of society that caused the current crisis. Underfunded regulatory agencies will struggle to compete for the most talented graduates and will have only a marginal impact on what those talented young people think is worth learning. We have learned many things from this crisis of course, and the best scholars will try, as they always have, to use those insights in their teaching and their research. But it will be an uphill struggle.

Nevertheless, there are certain improvements to curricula that would benefit everyone. I will discuss these under three headings: improvements for non-economists, improvements for undergraduate economists and improvements for postgraduate economists.

The first consists of improvements to general educational curricula (not just to economics courses). The teaching of basic statistics should be made a compulsory part of any student's learning programme, with less basic statistics for more advanced students even in humanities subjects. It can be made fun and it can be made rigorous at the same time (Ben Goldacre's excellent book *Bad Science* is a model of good practice in this respect). Simple cost–benefit analysis could also be considered a part of basic citizenship, not some geeky technique that only economists need to learn. In principle, there is no reason why these could not be taught much earlier, during secondary education. Although this might seem secondary to the question of what economists should be taught, it is worth making the point because it emphasizes the continuity between the skills of an economist and those of an educated and informed citizen.

But while non-economists need to learn a few techniques, economists should also be learning more than just techniques, and they should also be learning a more intuitive approach to the application of their techniques. Here are some suggestions.

(1) The teaching of statistics needs to be embedded in an understanding of empirical enquiry: what it is to do detective work on statistical data. This is hard to teach and must be done by example and not just by precept: through collecting real data and trying to understand what the data show and not just by reading a textbook. Sometimes it is as important to understand what should not be concluded from data as what can be: not every published paper reporting a t-statistic of two or more has in fact established what it claims in its abstract, for instance.

(2) Some economic history for economics students might have made the profession (and those in government and the private sector who listened to our messages) a bit more sceptical that we had banished the risk of crises for ever. Once again, it is not that economic history produces simple messages (it is striking, for instance, how much evolution there has been in our understanding of events in the 1930s through fairly recent research). One conclusion of good teaching in this area should be that it is often difficult to infer causality from historical events and that sometimes we need to be wary of messages like: 'the 1930s showed that…'.

(3) Including some behavioural economics in basic micro courses would also be desirable. The most important message of such work is not that 'people are irrational' but rather that 'people are very varied, and representative agent models miss many of the most important features of their interactions'.

(4) Perhaps, though, some microeconomic variant of the Lucas critique is the most important message of all for students to learn: as soon as regulators have a convincing model of the processes they are trying to regulate, some very smart people are going to set out to make money in ways that undermine the very assumptions of that model. Such phenomena are like predator–prey interactions in biology: studying these and other evolutionary processes may be a useful complement to the equilibrium modeling that is (deservedly) a dominant part of an economics education today.

(5) Following on from this, the most powerful improvement in economics education might be to find a way of teaching the subject that does not present it as an ever-more-successful approach to the truth about how economies work, but rather an investigation into a phenomenon that evolves as fast as we can keep up with it. This would require courses entitled something like 'Problems in economic analysis' that not only present the best current theory and evidence about a particular problem (such as competition policy, central banking, financial regulation, poverty) but also an overview of how our thinking has evolved with respect to the problem, an honest account of the false starts and confusions that have bedevilled the profession's attempts to get to grips with it, and some sense of what we still do not know. Such courses would not be easy to teach well.

Finally, if these are the desirable changes in undergraduate education, what do they imply about the teaching of postgraduates? These are, after all, the people who will teach future generations of undergraduates. The sheer technical challenge of much doctoral education means that many PhDs have not had the time or the energy to get much of a picture of the subject as a whole. One improvement might be to oblige PhD students to have a major and a minor field, not too closely related. But compulsion is unlikely to work, if only because incentives for PhD training can only be enforced by employers of PhDs. A better policy would be for the universities that are the employers of PhDs to announce that in recruiting on the job market they will look much more broadly than at the 'job market paper'. An excellent job market paper will be a necessary condition for recruitment but not a sufficient one. An ability to look beyond the candidate's main specialist field will be considered an important factor in determining how likely they are to be recruited. Of course, many top departments implicitly do this already, but it would be valuable if they signalled this more explicitly on the PhD job market.

Finance Is History!

By Harold James

A new sensitivity to the significance of historical experience has developed since the 2007 financial crisis. A recent report by the UK Chartered Financial Analyst Society castigates 'financial amnesia' among individuals, markets and regulators, and argues that 'it causes risk to be mispriced, bubbles to develop and crises to break'. The report suggests formal requirements for investment professionals to study financial history as a remedy.

Before the crisis, risk models were usually constructed on the basis of 'historical' data that covered only a relatively short time span: ten years, or often only five. The reasons for this are self-evident: beyond that limited range of dates, data comparability becomes a problem; current financial products do not have exact analogues in older trading instruments; regulatory practices have changed; and monetary policy is conducted in different ways. So history is bunk. Financiers thought that they had arrived at the 'end of history'.

After the crisis, there is a profound uncertainty, and no one can really be sure where they or the world is headed. So even rather odd and distant kinds of history might give some useful hints. In addition, professional financial agents are usually selling a particular product, and part of salesmanship is having a sales patter that has to sound informed. There is a premium on the ability to tell a story that for the moment captures the mood of the moment, but at other times will not (in the same way as men's suits can have lapels that are too wide or too narrow, and women can have skirts that are too long or too short, for the fashion of the hour). History can be a randomly mined source of fairy tales.

Incidentally, the new-found interest in history in the middle of doubt, uncertainty and crisis is a relatively constant feature of the human mind. That proclivity works in politics, where historical analogues are often the last resort of the truly desperate. For instance, in the last days of the Second World War, Adolf Hitler conjured up memories, as retold by Thomas Carlyle, of the miraculous victories of the Prussian king Frederick the

Great. But it is also true of finance. In the Great Depression, after October 1929, Americans suddenly became interested in the crash of 1907; just as in 1907 they had recalled the panic of 1876.

What exactly do people in a very different present want to get out of a rather remote past? There are three possible ways of using or abusing the past.

First, there is history as a source of *patterns*. This is presumably what the Chartered Financial Analyst Society was primarily thinking of when it recommended more history lessons. History can offer a better knowability of outcomes. It can offer a sophisticated set of precedents that simply appear as analogies, without really providing any explanations of why the parallels should exist. In a similar way, there was always an uncertainty about why the pattern detection beloved by technical stock analysts or chartists would really work. Is that because there is a mass psychology that obeys particular laws, just as the interactions of particles in fluids or gases create laws of motion (which are also often now studied as holding analogies to the interactions of milliards of individual decisions in financial markets)? Or is it because enough people also believe in the same fundamentally irrational pattern behaviour to make that—by the fact of an adequate numbers of devotees of technical analysis—a self-fulfilling prophecy? Some of the most influential recent writing on crises fits exactly into the latter mould. Carmen Reinhart and Kenneth Rogoff, for instance, tell us that downturns that involve banking crises are longer than recessions with no banking crises, and they give us average lengths for the duration of downturns.

Second, undoubtedly the most common use of history in financial crises is that history can be a source of *policy advice*. It can instil a sense of how predictable (or otherwise) policy outcomes are. This was a practice even in the heady years of the boom at the turn of the millennium, when some central bankers were using history to warn of the possibility of deflation and depression. In the aftermath of the 2007 crisis, the policy-related use of history is very common. Immediately after the collapse of Lehman Brothers there was a broad consensus, built on historical interpretation, that counter-cyclical fiscal and monetary policy could stop a Great Depression. Old schools of Keynesians and monetarists might give different types of advice, but they both depended on the idea that there were macroeconomic policy lessons from the 1930s.

In responding to the crisis, monetary policy did indeed contribute to a stabilization of expectations in 2009, but the aftermath of the fiscal stimuli has been disappointing. The US stimulus package was seen as necessary to reduce unemployment rates below 9%. Judged by that goal, it has not been effective. The Chinese 4 trillion renminbi stimulus kept growth going but at the cost of an asset and bank bubble that is now bursting. European countries were urged by the European Union and by other countries—notably the United States—to coordinate stimulus. But that only made many of them vulnerable when the sustainability of sovereign debt was reassessed.

There are several policy quandaries in which long-term stabilization goals appear to conflict with short-term recovery objectives. In each case, there is a Great Depression analogy.

Monetary policy is constrained in many countries by exchange rate choices. The members of the Eurozone threw away the exchange rate as a tool of policy when they signed up, just as those countries that returned to the ties of the Gold Standard in the 1920s did. But ending that commitment would lead to a revaluation of liabilities and would increase debt burdens that are already regarded as intolerable. So both staying in the commitment mechanism and exiting it are unbearably painful choices.

Fiscal arithmetic produces analogous dilemmas. We do not know how to handle the fiscal issues posed by the financial crisis. Doubts about the sustainability of government debt produce sudden surges in interest rates, as risk premia rise dramatically with perceptions of the likelihood of default. Such rises do not take place in a linear way, but occur with great suddenness. For countries on the brink, a perverse logic follows. Government debt service had in general become easier because of the low-interest-rate environment. But hints of new fiscal imprudence or of the abandonment of plans for long-term debt consolidation and reduction would drive up borrowing costs dramatically. In those circumstances, the additional costs of debt service easily outweigh any gains that might come from some measure of fiscal relaxation.

Moreover, as in some countries in the Depression era, contagion is magnified by the consequences of banking instability and crisis. In the summer of 1931, a series of bank panics emanated from central Europe and spread financial contagion, first to Great Britain, then to the United States and France, and then to the whole world. This financial turmoil was decisive in turning a bad recession (from which the United States was already clearly recovering in the spring of 1931) into the Great Depression.

Finding a way to repair the damage was very tough in the 1930s and is just as difficult now. There are no obvious macroeconomic answers to financial distress. The answers, if they exist, lie in the slow and painful cleaning up of balance sheets, and in designing an incentive system that compels banks to operate less dangerously and to take fewer risks. But cleaning up banks immediately makes them likely to reduce lending, thus exacerbating the downturn. Consequently, in each country there is a convoluted debate about whether a bank clean-up is really needed just now. Though there is some discussion of financial sector reform, with a gradual consensus building around sliding or incremental capital adequacy rules, many systemically important banks became bigger rather than smaller as a result of the crisis.

Third, history shows us something about the multiple *possibilities* of any given moment. In technical language, it constantly tells us multiple equilibria stories. Debt can be sustainable for long periods with low interest rates, but when some unexpected development occurs, and rates rise, previously manageable debt ratios become unmanageable. Members of the Eurozone are currently going through exactly this process of discovering that notions of sustainability can be very fragile. In the European case, there is no pattern, and no real chance either of assessing developments on the basis of calculated probabilities, but rather simply an awareness of the fragility of all calculations.

A simple-minded application of historical lessons can provide a really bad policy guide. It does not offer self-evident patterns either. The best way of thinking about history is as a way of testing conventional hypotheses—particularly when those hypotheses are being used to create market opportunities (by building false confidence, but also by engendering exaggerated despair). Conventional thinking offers—in financial debates as in others—a primrose path to perdition. Clio's task is to show us that it is not the only path available.

PART 3

MACROECONOMICS AFTER
THE CRISIS

Reforming the Macroeconomics Curriculum

By Wendy Carlin

In the course of revising a macroeconomics textbook, which was first published in 2006, recent events have made it clear to me that the current curriculum has some shortcomings (Carlin and Soskice 2006). Thinking about how to teach macroeconomics to undergraduates after the crisis led me to reflect on how macro is taught now and how the current curriculum became embedded. The outcome will be a new rather than a revised book (Carlin and Soskice 2013).

The undergraduate curriculum should be seen in the context of the basic curriculum for MSc students, which consists of the neoclassical growth model, to which rational expectations and technology shocks are added to derive the real business cycle model. With the further addition of money and sticky prices, the familiar New Keynesian dynamic stochastic general equilibrium three-equation model emerges. The emphasis is on a unified stochastic growth and business cycle model and this can be seen in the left-hand side of figure 13.1. Undergraduate courses are typically broader, as shown in the right-hand side of the figure. Market imperfections are often at the core of both the 'IS', or aggregate demand, and the 'PC' (for Phillips curve), or supply, blocks. In both cases, the curriculum sets out a paradigm that provides a theoretical underpinning for the Taylor rule regime for macroeconomic policy based on inflation-targeting central banks. The monetary rule is shown as the 'MR' schedule in the figure. But in both versions, the financial sector does not appear at all.

Given this curriculum, students were poorly equipped to understand either the unfolding of the credit crunch or the deeper roots of the financial crisis and the Great Recession that has followed. This period has exposed how we failed to educate students on important topics such as economic history and on the relevance of financial markets to macroeconomics. Economic history should include an appreciation of how economic thinking about macroeconomics has evolved, as well as knowledge of historical episodes, shifts in policy regimes and recent economic

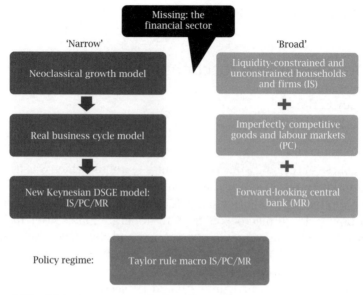

Figure 13.1. Mainstream macro before the crisis.

events. The perspective of alternative traditions such as the Austrian school can be included under this heading. Admittedly, however, it is easier to insist on what should be added in rather than to decide on what should be left out of a crowded syllabus.

It might be useful, therefore, to consider surveys of what is now taught, in order to see whether there is scope to make space in the curriculum. In a survey of 768 undergraduate economics instructors in the United States and Europe conducted in December 2010 (34% response rate), Gaertner *et al.* (2011) found that

- some version of aggregate demand/aggregate supply (or the broad three-equation model sketched above) is virtually universal in the courses taught by those surveyed;
- real business cycle models and the New Keynesian Phillips curve are taught in 70–75% of mandatory macro courses;
- there is now more coverage of public debt dynamics than there was pre-crisis;
- the biggest difference between courses in the United States and in Europe is that coverage of banks and financial institutions is much more prevalent in US courses than it is in those in Europe;

- there was also a greater tendency in Europe to say that topics in banking and finance introduced because of the crisis did not belong in the macro course; and
- there has been an increased emphasis on economic history and on case studies since the crisis.

In short, the teaching of undergraduate macroeconomics has in practice already been extended somewhat post-crisis, and we therefore face the challenge of expanding the already crowded curriculum. How can this problem be tackled?

One response is to teach models with more context by explaining the interconnections among the paradigm, the policy regime and events such as the crisis. This is preferable to teaching 'thought' and 'history' as add-ons that require additional time and do not anchor models to the context of their time.

For example, having set out the three-equation model and the associated inflation-targeting policy regime (as in the right-hand side of figure 13.1), we can ask where the Taylor rule macro paradigm and policy regime came from and how did it become dominant? The 'new consensus macroeconomics' paradigm, and its policy regime of a Taylor rule applied by inflation-targeting central banks, arose as a response to the inflation crises of the 1970s: the ultimate empirical failure of earlier Keynesian models. This Taylor rule policy approach was followed by two decades of growth and stability that became known as the Great Moderation. However, it is now clear with hindsight that the paradigm did not incorporate a number of phenomena that proved to be the seeds of the global financial crisis. They include

- the effects on financial fragility of financial liberalization,
- low unemployment but rising inequality in a labour market whose middle-rung jobs were being 'hollowed out', and
- interdependent global growth patterns: export-based (e.g. China, Germany) and finance-based (e.g. United States, United Kingdom).

The recent crisis has thus highlighted the shortcomings of the new consensus macroeconomics paradigm that still forms the basis of the curriculum, especially the absence of an integrated treatment of money, credit and international financial imbalances. One of the lessons we should take from this is that the study of financial markets should not be separated from macroeconomics, but should instead be incorporated into the economic models that students are taught. With our current

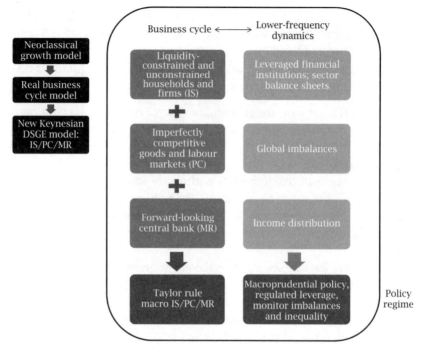

Figure 13.2. The future of macroeconomics in undergraduate economics.

perspective on recent history, we can see that the Taylor rule policy regime was consistent with low inflation but allowed excessive leverage and financial imbalances to occur. Inattention to the 'paradox of credibility' allowed a Minsky-type crisis to occur.

Another useful (earlier) example of the link between a macro paradigm and its policy regime is the Great Depression of the 1930s, which led to the dominance of the Keynesian paradigm in the post-war era. Just as in the 1990s and 2000s the Taylor rule regime followed the crisis of the mid 1970s, that earlier global economic crisis was followed by a major shift in macroeconomic thinking and policymaking. Improved macro-economic performance on the basis of Keynesian demand-management models followed, and the improvement was linked by many commentators to the change of policy regime. But did the improved macroeconomic performance that was seen as a result of each successive new policy regime contain the seeds of a new source of instability that had the potential to incubate the next global crisis? Figure 13.2 sketches a cycle of crisis, paradigm change, policy reaction, improved macro performance—and the seeds of the next crisis. Global economic crises are rare events; this

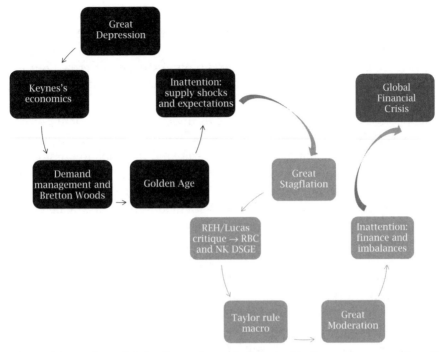

Figure 13.3. Where did the Keynesian paradigm and policy regime come from?

cycle of shifts in paradigm and related policy regime occurs infrequently. Setting out these connections can give students some perspective on the strengths and weaknesses of macro paradigms and the associated policy regimes and show how both are rooted in their historical context.

Using the broad interpretation of the mainstream that features in the undergraduate curriculum, the Taylor rule macro paradigm incorporated many of the insights of Keynesian economics from the previous paradigm. It combined them with better models of equilibrium unemployment, attention to credibility and the role of expectations, dynamics and sensitivity to the Lucas critique. The new paradigm and policy rule had beneficial macroeconomic results. However, we know now that there were important omissions in both the paradigm and the policy regime: the financial sector; the role of low-frequency dynamics such as those seen in leverage and income distribution (household and factor shares); and also the role of global imbalances. We clearly need to augment the Taylor rule macro of the business cycle with these elements, as shown in a new synthesis set out in figure 13.3 (this argument was set out initially in Carlin *et al.* (2012)).

In my view, it is important not to overreact to the recent crisis in reforming the macro curriculum. We need to guard against disempowering students by replacing modelling with nothing more than critique. A critique of models that have proved limited should not crowd out the teaching and application of the models themselves. The kind of approach and the synthesis set out above can help safeguard against this danger. At the MSc level, we should try not to undermine the students' broad framework for understanding the macroeconomy, and as they learn new modelling tools we should show them the kind of problems that quantitative model economies can help us understand. At the undergraduate level, we need to build better models than the simple three-equation one described earlier, yet we need to stick with models that can still be taught to undergraduates. At the same time, we can show undergraduates how learning, habit formation and adaptive behaviour can be captured by simple rules of thumb, and where these fit into a macro model. We should avoid treating these as fundamentally incompatible with our analytical macro framework.

Above all, we should teach humility, and the fallibility of models, using concrete historical and comparative examples, and explain how the learning that does arise as the result of something like the recent crisis can improve the paradigm and the policy regime. Macroeconomics and macro policy *have* improved over time. One example of improvement is the way that better understanding of models of oil shocks led to better policy. This is clear from comparing the contemporaneous analysis of and policy responses to OPEC I, OPEC II and the oil shock of 2002–8. Similarly, the lessons from the Great Depression in the United States *did* lead to better policy response in 2008–9, in relation to bank failures and the extension of liquidity by the Federal Reserve and central banks elsewhere. Equally, though, we should also show how lessons can be forgotten as a new paradigm takes hold. For example, some lessons of the 1930s were forgotten in the financial deregulation of recent times and in the neglect of the consequences of bank behaviour for sovereign debt. Similarly, the possibility of a liquidity trap in a depression was overlooked. More generally, lessons from recent experience in Japan and Latin America were too easily dismissed as of little relevance for the OECD economies in trouble now.

Although standard macro courses do need to be extended, the incorporation of economic history and the parallel history of macro paradigms need not displace the teaching and application of an enriched macro model. On the contrary, it can be used to illustrate the historical cycle:

crisis → paradigm shift → new policy regime → seeds of next crisis.

In this framework there are plenty of useful things to teach and questions that students can sensibly tackle, and some examples are set out in the appendix below. We should make use of this crisis!

APPENDIX: SAMPLE EXAM QUESTIONS

(1) Using the models you have studied in this course and reflecting on the recent experience of the Eurozone, analyse the macroeconomic issues at stake in the call for Scottish independence from the United Kingdom.

(2) Using the models you have studied in this course, explain how the contrasting growth strategies of globally important economies could lead to growing current account imbalances whilst inflation remained stable in each country. Would you expect the world real interest rate to increase, decrease or remain unchanged? Explain your reasoning.

(3) 'The use of fiscal stabilization policy in response to a fall in aggregate demand always leads to a government debt crisis.' Evaluate this claim referring to both theory and evidence.

(4) Using a model, explain why the externality imposed by the risk of a bank failure is of macroeconomic significance.

(5) Using the models you have studied, explain the argument that shifts in income distribution could have played a role in the genesis of (a) the stagflation crisis of the 1970s and (b) the present global financial crisis.

REFERENCES

Carlin, W., and D. Soskice. 2006. *Macroeconomics: Imperfections, Institutions, and Policies.* Oxford University Press.

Carlin, W., and D. Soskice. 2013. *Macroeconomics: Finance, Stability, and Crises.* Oxford University Press (forthcoming).

Carlin, W., R. J. Gordon and R. M. Solow 2012. Round table discussion: where is macro going? In *What's Right with Macroeconomics?* (ed. R. M. Solow and J.-P. Touffut). Cheltenham: Edward Elgar (forthcoming).

Gärtner, M., B. Griesbach and F. Jung. 2011. Teaching macroeconomics after the crisis: a survey among undergraduate instructors in Europe and the US. Discussion Paper 2011-20, Universität St Gallen (May).

Some Really Useful Macroeconomics

By Jagjit S. Chadha

In this chapter I argue that, far from abandoning the neoclassical agenda, the financial crisis should motivate the economics profession to work harder to integrate a number of insights from an earlier generation of models for use in micro-founded macroeconomic models. The ongoing crisis has encouraged calls for a fundamental rethink of macroeconomic models. But rather than driving us to develop ad hoc approaches, the well-known limitations of the basic New Keynesian monetary policymaking paradigm can be supplemented with tried and tested models that would have given us useful policy insights ahead of the crisis, had they been used. I illustrate here two obvious avenues that need integration into the basic model. One concerns how the so-called global savings glut affected neutral real rates. The other is how exchange rates and domestic demand are closely linked by the need to achieve domestic and external balance.[1] I conclude with a discussion of some changes that are needed to the incentives faced by academic economists to help bridge the gap between research and policy.

The ongoing financial crisis has injected a great deal of uncertainty into the economic belief system. In the eyes of many people, it would appear that an economic crisis necessarily implies a crisis in economics itself. So much so, in fact, that many are not only questioning the relevance of trying to use microeconomic foundations in order to understand economic behaviour in the aggregate, but are even also ascribing a causal role to the overreliance on such economic models, or on one type of economic model, as a contributory factor in the crisis. In this short chapter I will argue that although there *was* too much reliance on one type of simple

This material was prepared for the conference 'What Post-Crisis Changes Does the Economics Discipline Need?', which was held on 7 February 2012 at the Bank of England and which was co-organized with the Government Economic Service. I am grateful for comments from Alan Beath, Alan Carruth, Diane Coyle, Sean Holly, Dave Ramsden, Danny Quah and Richard Smith and I apologize to Willem Buiter for my chapter title.

[1] See Bernanke (2005) and Metzler (1960) on the global savings and investment schedules and Meade's (1951) precursor of the Salter–Swan diagram.

model, the methodology implied by that model has in no way been shown to be flawed.

In fact, the challenge faced by economists really stems from two basic errors. The first error was to over-analyse the policy implications of a simple New Keynesian model in which the only source of rigidity was some form of price stickiness. The second was to compound the problem by expending extensive resources trying to estimate forms of this toy-model and then using those models to underpin policy formulation, rather than developing a more convincing structure in which informational and financial frictions trigger significantly different responses to economic shocks. These errors made it nearly impossible to develop a richer vein of models, resulting in the kind of policy prescriptions that were chosen—in a hurry and in the dark—in response to this crisis.

Let us look briefly at the policy choices made after the crisis. We discovered that monetary policy is not only *theoretically* constrained at the lower zero bound interest rate: it really is constrained, and interest rate rules were therefore not able to stabilize an economy in all states of nature.[2] This led to the rediscovery of the importance of using open market operations to try and influence important key interest rates in the monetary transmission mechanism. We discovered that fiscal policy operates not only to help aggregate demand but also to recapitalize banks, therefore becoming a fiscal backstop not only for the real economy but also for the financial sector, which is subject to its own borrowing constraints. We found that banks, as highly geared maturity transformers, had insufficient liquidity in the event of an increase in risk aversion. They needed to be required to do so by regulation. The central bank used balance sheet operations to expand the size and composition of its balance sheet, to reduce the duration of financial markets' bond holdings and to increase liquidity. These operations involved the issuance of short-term fiscal instruments (interest rate bearing reserves or Treasury Bills) so that a 'monetary–fiscal operation' was used to hedge liquidity risk. Overall, policymakers discovered that it was not so much the level of the bank rate that mattered but the whole 'monetary–fiscal–financial mix'. As I have argued elsewhere, the Science of Monetary Policy had to be replaced with the Art of Central Banking.[3]

---

[2]Charlie Bean argued in careful and guarded analysis in 2003 that we might expect to lie at the zero bound around 2% at the time (Bean 2003).

[3]See Chadha and Holly (2011, p. 3) for an assessment of the first dynamic stochastic general equilibrium art and policy responses to the crisis over the period 2009–10.

For a decade after the adoption of central bank independence, we became accustomed to one interest rate being used to stabilize inflation by inducing aggregate demand to converge with capacity. In fact, by the middle of the noughties, policymakers were considering how to make this simple process even more transparent and simple with policy guidance; they even published interest rate forecasts intended to help people learn about the transition path. The promise of 'no more boom and bust'[4] and the creation of a spurious degree of certainty about the path of policy rates contributed to the overall sense that a substantial quantity of business cycle risk had been eliminated. This probably encouraged further excessive risk taking both by financial institutions and by the household sector.

However, it would be an error to drop the promising agenda of micro-founded models. These deal with the Lucas critique, develop policy prescriptions that take into account expectations and the structure of the economy, and embed policy responses in agents' actions. They therefore allow us to make welfare calculations about the consequences of different policy choices. Many of the analytical and policy mistakes that were made during the crisis can be analysed without necessarily requiring wholesale reform of the economics agenda.

In the next section, I will briefly outline the simple New Keynesian paradigm and consider the implications of informally relaxing some of its uncertainties, specifically over the 'natural rate'. I will then briefly consider how policy might have been different if some of the factors we now consider important had been given the correct weight in real time. One fundamental lesson that emerges is that what academics need to do is not so much rethink the subject, but, rather more prosaically, engage more in the policy debate.

THE MODELS

The Basic New Keynesian Policymaker

New Keynesian economists had figure 14.1 at the back of their minds when thinking about monetary policy. There is an inflation target where the dotted line meets the horizontal axis. When we add back in the natural rate of interest or the neutral real interest rate, we arrive at the steady-state policy rate: this is where the dotted line meets the vertical axis.

---

[4]This phrase, or a variant of it, was used often by Gordon Brown and other members of the New Labour administration, and even appeared in the letter granting operational independence to the Bank of England in May 1997.

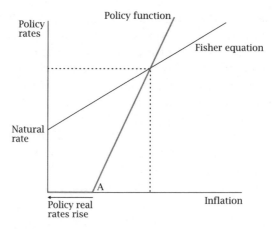

Figure 14.1. The New Keynesians.

The line labelled 'Fisher equation' simply adds a nominal return onto the natural rate of interest defined at the expected inflation rate, which for the purposes of simplicity we set equal to the actual inflation rate plus some random error. All points along the Fisher equation line imply the same real or neutral real interest rate and do not therefore impact on aggregate demand, which is a negative function of deviations in the policy rate from this real rate. Perturbations from aggregate demand relative to supply lead to inflation (not shown on the chart). The policy function is therefore steeper than the Fisher equation line and it brings aggregate demand down when there is upward inflationary pressure and vice versa (this figure is developed from first principles in Chadha (2008)).

In this rather mechanistic setting we can understand the impact of, for example, changes to the natural rate, which implies a shift up in the point where the Fisher equation meets the axis and also a shift upwards and to the left for the policy function at a given inflation rate. We can also easily understand why a mistaken belief that the natural rate, which cannot be observed, has not changed can lead rather quickly to problems as policy rates may be left too low for too long, excessively stimulating demand. Whilst the possibility of uncertainty about the natural rate was clear, we were unable to say anything very much about how to identify changes in it or even think in a constructive manner about the correct set of market interest rates that might allow us to understand the neutral rate.[5]

---

[5]Given that inflation may respond with a lag to current and expected output gaps, rather than being rational and forward looking, mistakes in measuring the output gap can have similarly deleterious consequences.

Still, setting aside the two great real-time unmeasurables—the output gap and the neutral rate of interest—it seemed that inflation, and aggregated demand relative to supply, could be stabilized if policy was sufficiently forward looking. At the point marked A in figure 14.1, though, things change. Here, nominal rates cannot fall with inflation, and ever-larger negative output gaps, driving down inflation, will thereby increase real rates and so, in principle, set-up a destabilizing feedback loop—unless something else can be found to ease monetary and financial conditions. These instruments turned out to be first a large depreciation in the exchange rate and then, with more novelty, quantitative easing.

Elsewhere (Chadha 2010), I have listed a number of well-documented causes of the crisis.

   (i) A long business cycle expansion, leading to (temporarily) self-fulfilling prophecies of stability or moderation.

  (ii) A saving glut (mainly Asian savings) that sent capital flowing to high-consumption societies, lowered required rates of return and inflated asset prices.

 (iii) A boom in financial engineering that was able to create liquidity and excessive levels of bank leverage.

 (iv) Monetary and fiscal policy that ran the domestic economy at more than full capacity, in the belief that inflation was the only indicator of macroeconomic health, even as inflation itself was increasingly providing a misleading signal.

  (v) A regulatory framework that was not sufficiently aware of risk in the whole system, and a system of bank regulation that did not fully understand the trading picture or the capital structure of the institutions it supervised.

What I am attempting to do here is walk a tricky tightrope. I want to argue not that the paradigm of micro-founded macro models is wrong *per se* but rather that a far richer model structure is required. This does not require us to talk about banks. Instead, I will illustrate this argument with two models that come from the postwar Bretton Woods period but should arguably have more fully informed both macro-modelling and the policy debate.[6]

---

[6]There are examples of other models that might be usefully reexamined, such as Mundell–Fleming, as well as deeper issues connected with money and liquidity.

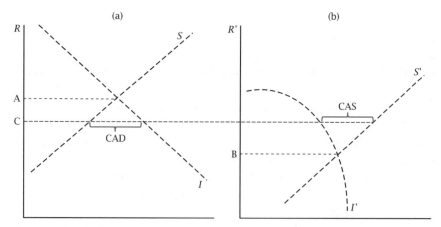

Figure 14.2. Global imbalances and real rates. (a) Debtor countries: savings and investment. (b) Creditor countries: savings and investment.

The Metzler Diagram

In the long run, real rates can be expected to adjust to equilibrate the pool of savings and planned investment (this section draws on Chadha (2012)). In a global economy, capital outflows should tend to go from saver countries that are wealthy to poorer countries with limited savings but abundant investment opportunities. One of the root causes of the financial crisis has been the unnatural sight of capital flowing 'uphill': that is, from poor countries to rich ones. In a famous calculation, Robert Lucas showed that if a rich country and a poor one have equivalent production technologies and differ only in income per head, then because the amount of capital employed in the poorer country will be less than in the richer country, the marginal efficiency of capital must be higher in the poorer country and that country should therefore attract capital (Lucas 1990). For example, Chinese per capita income is around $5,000 at the purchasing power parity exchange rate and that in the United States is around $45,000, implying that the rate of return on capital in the United States should be a small fraction, around 3–4%, of that in China.[7] That should then mean that China runs a current account deficit financed by a US capital surplus. The reality, of course, has been the obverse, with the United States recycling China's capital flows.

---

[7]The return on capital in the United States ought to be such a small fraction of that in a poorer country because its output per head is so much higher (nine times higher than in China, for example). So considerably more capital per head is employed in the United States, which implies a lower marginal rate of return with decreasing returns to scale.

Global savings equal investment at a single world interest rate (ignoring risk). Figure 14.2 draws the equilibria for both autarchy (points A and B) and a two-country world (point C) given their respective savings and investment schedules. If the debtor country and the creditor country are both closed economies, in the debtor country (figure 14.2(a)) real interest rates (R) would clear the domestic market for saving above A and the equilibrium level for savings (S) and investment (I) would be determined accordingly. This would represent the natural rate drawn in figure 14.1. Overseas, in the saver economy (see figure 14.2(b)), the higher level of savings at any given interest rate and the lower investment demand would imply, if there were no capital mobility from saver nations to borrower nations, that the real rate there would fall to B with savings and investment clearing internally.[8]

This explains why, in the absence of perfect capital flows, real interest rate differences may persist, as real rates will depend on domestic savings and investment schedules alone. But when we open up to capital flows when interest rates initially stand at A and B, the debtors will expand investment demand relative to savings and run a current account deficit (CAD) at some intermediate interest rate between A and B (let us say C), and the creditor nations will generate a current account surplus (CAS) to meet the debtors' demands. The surplus (respectively, deficit) in each year adds to (respectively, reduces) net foreign assets in each year in the creditor (respectively, debtor) country and leads to an increasing stock of claims by the surplus nations on the debtor nations.

The counterpart of 'excess' savings in creditor nations is 'excessive' (private and public) investment in the debtor nations. So, might small reductions in debtor country demand (investment) provide the answer? That will indeed be part of the necessary adjustment, but it will not necessarily be enough. Even if demand falls sufficiently with an inward shift in the investment demand function (labelled 'I' in the figure), to eliminate the debtor's current account deficit at stable world rates (C), creditors would still have excess savings. This excess would drive rates down from C and would lead to the reemergence of a current account deficit, albeit with lower world rates and a lower level of global imbalances. Obviously, large enough falls in debtor demand will achieve zero current account balances in both countries at very low real interest rate and low market clearing levels of debtor country savings and investment. Perhaps this is

---

[8]I have drawn the investment schedule for saver nations as concave to the origin to try and capture capacity constraints and domestic difficulties in financial intermediation.

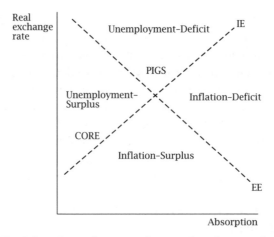

Figure 14.3. The Salter–Swan diagram of internal and external equilibrium.

the outcome, as we stare at a prolonged global slowdown, that we are actually heading towards?

There are two points to take from this model. First, that global savings schedules may loosen domestic financial conditions, and so imply a higher neutral real rate, due to lower market interest rates, and this will help to elevate asset prices and support debt-financed consumption. Increasing policy rates earlier would tend to act against this process. Second, the accrual of international debt suppresses future demand below the level it would otherwise have reached and so will act to depress demand for a long period, which may or may not be an optimal response. Models therefore need financial conditions to be articulated and they need choices on the optimal quantity of debt to be formalized.[9]

The Salter–Swan diagram

The Salter–Swan analysis of open economies is another model that might help to illuminate the Eurozone problem. Set out in figure 14.3, it plots an external equilibrium locus (EE) with the required real exchange rate as a negative function of domestic demand, or absorption, and the internal equilibrium locus (IE) with the required real exchange rate as a positive function of absorption. This was the classic model that was used

---

[9]In most early dynamic stochastic general equilibrium models, debt either represents inside money and nets out in aggregate or, if it is public debt, it is treated as Ricardian and therefore does not impact on net wealth.

to think about the problems of the Bretton Woods era and it therefore has some relevance for the Eurozone. Countries with excessive levels of demand (absorption) relative to their capacity (or productivity) levels—the so-called PIGS (Portugal, Italy, Greece, Spain), for example—are likely to suffer from external payments deficits and, if their real exchange rate is too high, also from unemployment. The creditor nations in the Eurozone, 'CORE', lie to the left of the EE curve as they have some degree of unemployment but run surpluses. If there is unemployment in every country, then the whole Eurozone will benefit from a lower real exchange rate. All these nations might also benefit from a structural transfer mechanism, as it might not be the case that the same countries always lie to the left or the right of the EE locus.[10] Overall, if deficits are consistently balanced by creditors, the zone as a whole lies on the EE curve and, with a depreciation, on the intersection with the IE locus as well. The story of the chart is simply that some combination of changes to the path of domestic absorption and the real exchange rate should allow any country or set of countries to achieve both internal and external equilibrium. Only if the scale of one country's overhang is large enough, or persistent enough, to prevent adjustment will some form of debt restructuring be required.

Policy

I do not want to get into the blame game concerning the macroeconomic and financial risks that built up during the long expansion, which started in 1992, and became manifest during the financial crisis. Recessions are an unfortunate part of macroeconomic fluctuations and will always offer a challenge to both economic theory and policy practice. Here I want to note that, even as micro-founded models were groping around for a satisfactory way to model financial conditions or the importance of balance sheets and credit constraints, there were available analytical frameworks that allowed us to think about the impact of global imbalances and the open economy on the domestic interest rate decision. They could usefully have been used to think hard about the conjuncture ahead of the crisis. The recycling of savings from abroad reduced global real interest rates and meant that for any given stance of monetary policy, financial conditions were looser than they would otherwise have been. This ought

---

[10]Although clearly it has been the case that member countries do not have debtor or creditor status at random, and the transfers are expected to be in the same direction semi-permanently, which may build up an unsustainable stock of claims.

to have been a clearer signal of the impending crisis to policymakers, particularly as it was associated with rapid broad money growth, escalating house prices and increasing levels of household indebtedness.[11] The necessary analytical tools were available. It was not necessary to rethink the methodology of economic models, but some encouragement should perhaps have been given to relax some aspects of the models and think a little about where we needed to go, using some of the key experiences of the past.

Concluding Remarks

Academic economists have many calls on their time. Teaching quality has rightly been given much attention, as both the level and intensity of interest in studying economics have been given considerable impetus by the financial crisis. There has been a 'good' distributional shock as young people are choosing economics at the expense of other social sciences.[12] Yet research is both inherently time consuming and, because of the need to meet the rules of the research assessment game, directed towards an agenda set by a small number of mostly US-based journals. This objective does not provide a great incentive for UK-based academics to study the UK economy! The average cycle of reviews and revisions took around two years in 2001 (see Ellison 2002) for the small proportion of submitted papers that were eventually published. Unfortunately, there is very little evidence to suggest that the length of this cycle has fallen. With the need to publish four papers in a 4–5 year window to satisfy the requirements of the Research Assessment Exercise, it leaves very little time to contribute to UK-based policy discussions.

Rather than calling for new tracts of yet-undigested economic science, I would rather see more attention paid to key insights from existing research. There are around a dozen winners of the Nobel Memorial Prize in Economic Sciences whose work would make a pretty good start for any

---

[11] Salter–Swan can also give some insights about the United Kingdom. If absorption is too high, leading to an external deficit, but there is no domestic inflation, then we are likely to lie on the IE locus northeast of equilibrium. And this suggests that as well as excessive absorption, the real exchange rate is too high and should have been allowed or encouraged to fall. This would have reduced, at least to some degree, the dependence on ever-cheaper imported manufactured goods to help meet the inflation target.

[12] The Economics Network at the University of Bristol has produced work to suggest that the premium from studying economics is high relative to that from studying other social science or humanity degrees, particularly for women.

macroeconomics course. More attention should also be given, perhaps, to the teaching of economic and financial history. By this I do not mean economic thought. The sterile debate about what Keynes really meant should be left to some more arcane part of academe than economics departments. We should want to ensure that the next generation of economists not only understand some of the causes of this crisis but also understand that crises, recessions and crashes are part of the subject and not its death knell. This would entail improving the incentives for academics to work on critical literature reviews, on financial and economic history and directly on policy questions by rating such work far more highly in the Research Excellence Framework.

I am often told that there is a failure of academic economists in the United Kingdom to involve themselves in the wider public debate, albeit with one or two honourable exceptions. Academic economists have little incentive to do so, however. The public understanding of economics does seem to be rather poor and we are almost universally regarded as forecasters or even soothsayers rather than as careful research-based thinkers. It is as hard to explain the subtleties of neuroscience as the complications of setting monetary policy in a two-minute sound bite. It seems to me that the journalists who report on economics rarely seem to be fans of the discipline, which might not be unconnected with our rather insular academic professional practice. But, as we know and teach, behaviour responds to incentives. Perhaps we need more formalized exchanges between economics departments and employers of economists from the undergraduate level to the mature academic level. I would certainly like to offer an ongoing outreach programme to tired members of the Government Economic Service or the Bank of England to spend time at an economics department so that we can learn from one another.

Economists are, of course, far from perfect—particularly macroeconomists. As someone who is regularly dazzled by the genius of my game theoretic colleagues, I am frequently made to feel like a lower specimen on the evolutionary scale. Alas, we cannot all be virtuosi and macroeconomists need to focus on policy questions. And yet the science, as it stands, is subject to the same fads, fashions and futility that invade any other aspect of human endeavour. But rather like the music back catalogue, there are some favourites that we should all keep in our heads, if only to ensure we do not forget what we once knew. They give us a starting point to think about current policy dilemmas and try to persuade the public at large that the profession really does have something worthwhile to say.

REFERENCES

Bean, C. 2003. Asset prices, financial imbalances and monetary policy: are inflation targets enough? In *Asset Prices and Monetary Policy* (ed. A. Richards and T. Robinson). Reserve Bank of Australia Annual Conference Volume. Sydney: Reserve Bank of Australia.

Bernanke, B. S. 2005. The global saving glut and the US current account deficit. Remarks delivered during the Homer Jones Lecture.

Chadha, J. S. 2008. Monetary policy analysis: an undergraduate toolkit. In *Macroeconomic Theory and Macroeconomic Pedagogy* (ed. G. Fontana and M. Setterfield). Palgrave Macmillan.

Chadha, J. S. 2010. The financial crisis: what have macroeconomists learnt? (Studium Generale Lecture, Phillips-Universität Marburg.) In *Die Eskalation der Finanz-zur Wirtschaftskrise*. Fritz Knapp.

Chadha, J. S. 2012. World real interest rates: a tale of two regimes. DWS White Paper (February).

Chadha, J. S., and S. Holly (eds). 2011. *Interest Rates, Prices and Liquidity: Lessons from the Financial Crisis*. Cambridge University Press.

Ellison, G. D. 2002. The slowdown of the economics publishing process. *Journal of Political Economy* 110(5):947–993.

Lucas Jr, R. E. 1990. Why doesn't capital flow from rich to poor countries? *American Economic Review* 80(2):92–96.

Meade, J. E. 1951. *The Theory of International Economic Policy. Volume I: The Balance of Payments. Volume II: Trade and Welfare*. Oxford University Press/ Royal Institute of International Affairs.

Metzler, L. 1960. The process of international adjustment under conditions of full employment: a Keynesian view. Paper presented at the Econometric Society (December). (Reprinted, 1968, in *Readings in International Economics* (ed. R. E. Caves and H. G. Johnson). Homewood, IL: Irwin.)

Teaching Macroeconomics

By Roger E. A. Farmer

I have been teaching macroeconomics to undergraduate and graduate students for more than thirty years and over that period I have seen numerous changes in delivery, substance and style—not necessarily in that order. Since our undergraduate lecturers pass on what they themselves learn in graduate school, I will focus my attention in this article on the teaching of graduate economics. I would like to take this opportunity not only to say a little bit about pedagogy, but also to put my perceptions of the educational process in the context of the philosophy of science.

THE CORE OF ECONOMICS

Economics differs from most other social sciences, in that we economists share a common core body of knowledge and we indoctrinate our neophytes early. Every major graduate programme, throughout the world, is structured in the same way. The first year is devoted to an intensive study of three core subjects: microeconomic theory, macroeconomics and econometrics. At the end of the first year the students sit three comprehensive exams. Failure is not an option. A student who has not passed these exams after two tries is awarded a Master's degree and sent off into the real world.

The second year of the PhD programme is a little more relaxed, but still intense. Students continue to sit in taught lectures and, at this point, they specialize in two or more fields. At UCLA, we offer a 'breadth' option in which the third field is satisfied by choosing a selection of courses from different areas, one of which must be economic history or the history of thought. That requirement has been removed from some programmes—to the detriment of the schools that have abandoned it in my view.

THE HISTORY OF MACROECONOMIC IDEAS

Macroeconomics as a separate subject did not exist until after the publication of Keynes's master work *The General Theory of Employment, Interest and Money* in 1936. For thirty years after the Second World War, macro-economics was synonymous with the economics of Keynes and the same body of ideas was taught to graduate and undergraduate students alike. There were differences between alternative interpretations of Keynes: monetarism versus Keynesianism was one big debate. But even Milton Friedman, the father of modern monetarism, had a lot more in common with the Keynesians of his day than with what passes for macroeconomics today.

What happened? First, *The General Theory* is not an easy book to read. It is intellectually incoherent and contradictory in places. For example, the first part of the book assumes that wages are fixed but later chapters drop that assumption without providing a coherent theory of inflation. It was left to post-war Keynesians, notably Sir John Hicks in the United Kingdom and Alvin Hansen in the United States to interpret the theory. Their explanation of Keynesian economics was popularized by the father of American Keynesianism, Paul Samuelson, and taught to generations of economists who learned economics from Samuelson's textbook.

The Shift Away from Keynesianism in the 1970s

The post-war Keynesians closed Keynes's system by grafting onto it an empirical equation, the Phillips curve, that had been discovered by the New Zealander Bill Phillips. Phillips was a researcher at the London School of Economics. Samuelson called the integration of Keynesian ideas with the Phillips curve 'the neoclassical synthesis', and this has served as a practical guide to policymakers for thirty years. The theory predicted that stagflation—the coincidence of high inflation and high unemployment—was a theoretical impossibility. But in the 1970s we saw inflation rates climb above 10% while unemployment was approaching double digits. The post-war Keynesian consensus came crashing down in flames.

At this point, undergraduate and graduate classes in economics began to diverge. Most academic economists abandoned Keynesian ideas as the rational expectations revolution swept major universities. Rational expectations was a new research programme that reformulated macro-economic theory from scratch. It threw out the idea of involuntary unemployment that had been a hallmark of Keynesian economics. Instead, all right-thinking macroeconomists began to model labour markets with the assumption that the demand and supply of labour are always equal. As James Tobin famously quipped, the Great Depression was modelled as a sudden bout of contagious laziness.

The 1970s about turn in the macroeconomics curriculum was a major paradigm shift that occurred because Keynesian economics failed two important tests: one theoretical and one empirical. On the theoretical front, Keynes failed to explain why unemployed workers would not offer to work for a lower wage, and why profit-maximizing firms would fail to hire them. On the empirical front, Keynesian economics failed to explain stagflation. Either of these two failures on its own might not have been fatal, but together they led economists to go back to the drawing board and to rethink the foundations of their subject. As a consequence of the theoretical weakness and the empirical failure of Keynesian economics, macroeconomists reverted to the business cycle theory of the 1920s.

BACK TO THE FUTURE

In 1928, Arthur Pigou published a book, *Industrial Fluctuations*, that summarized the state of business cycle theory at the time. The business cycle theory of the 1920s contained six or more different causes of economic fluctuations. These included productivity shocks, agricultural disturbances, changes in tastes, industrial disputes, monetary shocks, news shocks and shifts in consumer confidence.

More recently, in the 1970s and 1980s, researchers (notably Finn Kydland and Ed Prescott) took the main ideas from Pigou and formalized them with mathematics in a programme known as real business cycle theory, or RBC theory for short. Because this programme was technically challenging, they simplified Pigou's theory to make the mathematics manageable. As my emeritus colleague Axel Leijonhufvud has observed, 'modern macroeconomics has become much like Hollywood movies; the pyrotechnics are spectacular but the plots are sadly lacking'.

It is easy to poke fun at the simplicity of early real business cycle theory, but it is hard to see how things might have evolved differently. The rational expectations revolution was the beginning of a movement in which macroeconomists learned to be more rigorous in the statement of their ideas. This is a process that began in microeconomics with the work of Walras, Pareto and Edgeworth in the nineteenth century. For macroeconomists, who deal with dynamic problems with uncertainty, the formalization could not have occurred earlier since the mathematical tools themselves were unavailable to earlier generations.

The introduction of more complex mathematics to graduate programmes in economics was not without consequences. It altered the kinds of student that we admitted and it dramatically increased the level of mathematical skills required to be admitted to a top programme. These changes had both advantages and disadvantages: on the plus side, PhD students who have graduated since 1980 have a much better grasp of how to formalize problems; on the minus side, many of them spend much less time learning about the history of thought or how to choose interesting problems in the first place.

WHAT HAS BEEN HAPPENING SINCE 1970?

The aftermath of the rational expectations revolution was a time of rediscovery in macroeconomics. Researchers schooled in the new mathematics began to discover the beauty of old ideas and, one by one, all of Pigou's six shocks have been formalized into a mathematical system of considerable intellectual elegance.

A group of New Keynesian economists rediscovered a role for monetary policy by adding frictions to the real business cycle model. In my own work with Jess Benhabib of New York University and Jang-Ting Guo of the University of California, Riverside, we put consumer confidence back into real business cycle models. Frank Portier of Toulouse University and Paul Beaudry of the University of British Columbia brought back news shocks. In 2006, on the eve of the Great Recession, macroeconomists made the not-insignificant achievement of formalizing 1920s business cycle theory using the mathematics of modern functional analysis.

In 2007, on the evening that Northern Rock went into bankruptcy, I was attending a conference dinner at the Bank of England. The conference was called to celebrate the Great Moderation, a term that was coined to describe the remarkable success of monetary policy in achieving a newfound economic stability using the tools of modern macroeconomic theory. The business cycle was declared to be conquered. We had entered a new era of economic prosperity in which the high priests of central bank research departments would divine the correct interest rate rules to maintain low inflation and high employment.

The reality was very different.

THE IMPACT OF THE CURRENT CRISIS

The collapse of Northern Rock heralded the start of the largest recession since the Great Depression of the 1930s. By the end of 2008, after the bankruptcy of Lehman Brothers, US unemployment had doubled from 5% to 10% and it has remained above 9% for twenty-two of the past twenty-four months. The US Treasury initiated an $800 billion fiscal stimulus and the Federal Reserve Open Market Committee increased the monetary base from $800 billion in the autumn of 2006 to its current value: close to $2,200 billion. But in spite of this remarkable bout of policy activism, things are getting worse, not better. The spectacular failure of the dominant paradigm to make sense of this situation has opened a door for alternative views of macroeconomics to enter the arena.

WHY IS PARADIGM CHANGE A RARE EVENT?

Although economics is a science, it is not an experimental science. At any point in time there are competing explanations of the same phenomena and the profession gravitates to what is perceived to be the most plausible. Since conflicts cannot be decided by appeal to experimental evidence, they are instead resolved by appeal to authority.

In normal times, influential thinkers at top universities control the progress of schools of thought. They control journals and what is published in those journals and they place their students in other elite institutions. Economists pursue rather narrow sets of ideas. There is considerable inertia in economic thought and new ideas are treated with scepticism.

Although that is frustrating for a creative theorist, it is hard to think of an alternative mechanism for disseminating ideas that would work more effectively. Inertia is important in a non-experimental science. It is simply too time consuming to waste social resources on the pursuit of every new idea that surfaces.

These are not normal times, however. Large disruptions in the economic environment—like the Great Depression of the 1930s, the stagflation of the 1970s and now the Great Recession of 2008—are difficult or impossible to understand within the existing paradigm. The Great Recession was a game-changing event of the same order of magnitude as stagflation and the Great Depression.

IN DEFENCE OF FORMALISM

Although it is possible to find fault with the teaching of modern macroeconomics, much of the reform of our subject that was introduced by the rational expectations school was useful and should be retained. During a 2009 visit to the London School of Economics, the Queen asked why economists had failed to predict the crisis. The Queen's remarks spawned a concerted attack on macroeconomics from journalistic luddites who criticized academic macroeconomists for wallowing in mathematical abstraction that has no connection with the real world. Some critics have gone further and argued for a repeal of the use of mathematics as part of an economics education. That is a bridge too far.

The crude real business cycle models of the last decade were wrong in important dimensions. But if a writer pens a bad novel, nobody argues that all writers should stop using paper and go back to clay tablets. Mathematics is the language of science and it has been essential for an understanding of modern economics since at least the turn of the nineteenth century. The use of mathematics in economics will not disappear, and nor should it.

Along with the teaching of mathematics, I would also defend the major principles of the rational expectations revolution. As Tom Sargent expressed it upon being awarded the 2011 Nobel Memorial Prize, rational expectations captures the notion popularized by Abraham Lincoln: 'You can fool some of the people all of the time or all of the people some of the time; but you can't fool all of the people all of the time.' That is a good idea and it deserves to remain.

WAS IT ALL A WASTE OF TIME?

We are standing on the same ground that Arthur Pigou, John Maynard Keynes, Friedrich von Hayek and Irving Fisher trod in 1929 and we are debating the same ideas. One could be forgiven for thinking that the intervening years were fruitless and that the rational expectations revolution was a waste of time. I do not hold that view.

Over the last thirty years we have learned how to incorporate the passage of time into our theories. As a direct consequence of the rational expectations revolution in macroeconomics, economists now know how to model the behaviour of forward-looking agents in environments that are both dynamic and stochastic—and we have learned how to analyse the response of those agents to proposed changes in policy.

On the applied front, we have developed methods for matching the theoretical predictions of our models to the data. Bayesian econometrics has made huge strides, mainly as a result of increased computing power. The invention of the digital computer has been a revolutionary event that will do for economics what the invention of the telescope did for astronomy.

The methods developed by real business cycle economists and by the rational expectations school are here to stay. But the fact that we have learnt how to construct dynamic stochastic models of interacting agents does not mean that we should accept the assumptions of the real business cycle school. We can and should use the sophisticated new building materials that have been provided for us, but we need not construct the same building.

A Personal Perspective on Reforming Macroeconomics

For every idea there is a season and we have returned to the season of Keynes. Just as Finn Kydland and Ed Prescott brought formal methods to the ideas of Pigou, so it is time to do the same for *The General Theory*. There is a branch of modern economics, New Keynesian economics, that claims to have done that. But as I have long argued, New Keynesian economics misses the central ideas and insights of *The General Theory*. These are that

(1) unemployment can persist as an equilibrium outcome of an unregulated capitalist economy and

(2) confidence is an independent driving force of business cycles.

These ideas are fundamental to an understanding of depressions and they are ideas that have been absent from macroeconomic thought for at least forty years.

I am not arguing that unemployment has been ignored by the profession. Far from it. The 2010 Nobel Memorial Prize was awarded to Chris Pissarides, Dale Mortensen and Peter Diamond for the theory that unemployment is caused by 'search frictions' in labour markets. But the important theoretical contribution of Diamond, Mortensen and Pissarides was not effectively integrated into the macroeconomic models that are used to guide policy.

Both New Keynesians and real business cycle economists continue to build models in which the quantities of labour demanded and supplied are always equal to each other. These models have been used by central banks and government economists to analyse economic policy for the past forty years. Yet in these models there *is no such thing* as unemployment.

There were also economists, myself included, who studied the role of confidence and self-fulfilling prophecies in generating business cycles. Just as the New Keynesians reintroduced money into the real business cycle model, so the literature on self-fulfilling prophecies reintroduced confidence. Both branches of the literature helped to provide a more complete mathematical version of Pigou's verbal theory of business cycles.

119

What was missing from previous work, including my own work on self-fulfilling prophecies in macroeconomics, was the recognition that unemployment can persist as a steady-state equilibrium.

When I connected that idea to the literature on self-fulfilling beliefs, I realized that it would lead to a profound change in the properties of our economic models. In conventional economic models, everything is driven by three fundamental forces: preferences, technology and endowments. To make sense of Keynesian insights, it is necessary to add confidence as an additional fundamental. Confidence becomes an independent driver of economic activity that can permanently increase the unemployment rate. That is one of the original contributions that I have formalized in my recent books (Farmer 2010a,b)). This line of enquiry leads to very different implications for the advice that policymakers should follow in order to restore full employment.

Three Proposals for the Reform of Graduate Macroeconomics

I have given a personal perspective on what needs to change. I also have some more general recommendations that I will state as three proposals for graduate programme reform.

First, to those schools that no longer teach economic history: reverse course. Integrate the teaching of history with the teaching of theory and use history to explain why our theories were developed in the first place. I have alluded to the disappearance of economic history from some departments. This is a process that I hope will be reversed in the coming years. Economic history is our data and it is as essential to economics as is a knowledge of the constellations to an astronomer.

Second, to those schools that do not teach the history of thought: reverse course. A knowledge of the history of economic ideas is essential to a non-experimental science because our research agendas often become diverted for the wrong reasons. Good ideas become forgotten and must be rediscovered. In physics and chemistry, ideas are discarded after their predictions are falsified in the face of repeated experiments. In economics, good ideas are sometimes discarded because they fall out of fashion.

That leads me to my final recommendation. There are very few empirical facts in macroeconomics. There are time series data that co-move in mysterious ways and there is a large set of theories that could potentially account for those co-movements. A knowledge of mathematics, statistics and econometrics is essential to understand this unfortunate reality.

Theory and measurement are conjoined twins and we must teach both to our graduate students if they are to have a hope of unravelling the mysteries of the social universe.

PROSPECTS FOR THE FUTURE

The macroeconomics of the last thirty years has consisted of rediscovering truths that were known to Pigou and his contemporaries in the 1920s. Gradually, real business cycle economists have reintroduced, one by one, the shocks that were known to our predecessors. Whereas 1920s theory was verbal, the macroeconomics of 2011 is formalized with a rigour that was not possible in 1928 because the mathematical tools did not exist.

In 2008, after the collapse of Lehman Brothers, we were hit with a similar catastrophe to the one that caused Keynes to give up on the framework of classical economics and develop *The General Theory*. The Great Depression was nursemaid to two important new ideas. The first is that high unemployment can persist forever as the steady state of a free market economy. The second is that confidence, which Keynes called 'animal spirits', is an independent force that drives business cycles. These insights were forgotten by several generations of Keynesians.

It is promising and significant that Keynes's two key ideas have now re-entered the discourse of modern macroeconomic theory. When they are integrated with the methods we have learnt from the rational expectations school, Keynes's insights have important implications for the way we should conduct macroeconomic policy in the twenty-first century. To a young macroeconomist about to start his or her career, that is a tremendously exciting prospect.

REFERENCES

Farmer, R. 2010a. *Expectations, Employment and Prices.* Oxford University Press.
Farmer, R. 2010b. *How the Economy Works: Confidence, Crashes, and Self-Fulfilling Prophecies.* Oxford University Press.

Rethinking Macroeconomics in the Wake of the Financial Crisis

By Benjamin M. Friedman

In 1772, at the height of the worst banking and economic crisis to hit Scotland in two generations, David Hume wrote to his friend Adam Smith. After recounting the bank closures, industrial bankruptcies and spreading unemployment the crisis had brought—reporting that 'even the Bank of England is not entirely free from Suspicion'—Hume asked: 'Do these Events any-wise affect your Theory?' They certainly did. As is evident in *The Wealth of Nations*, published just four years later, Smith took away the lessons of what his country had experienced and adapted his thinking accordingly.

Today's economists, including researchers as well as policymakers and teachers of the subject, likewise could usefully adapt their thinking in light of what happened in the financial crisis of 2007–9. The lessons of the crisis for macroeconomics are particularly striking, especially against the backdrop of the past several decades of dominant thinking within the field, which in light of the crisis looks not so much wrong as wrongheaded.

THE FINANCIAL INFLUENCE

In logical order, the first of those lessons is that financial phenomena have a powerful influence on output, employment and other dimensions of non-financial economic activity. On one level, everyone knows this. But a major direction of macroeconomic theorizing in recent decades has instead adopted the perspective that the economy's aggregate supply of

Parts of this chapter draw on two of my earlier papers: 'Reconstructing economics in light of the 2007–? financial crisis' from 2010 (*Journal of Economic Education* 41(4):391–397) and 'Struggling to escape from "assumption 14"' from 2012 (in *New Perspectives on Asset Price Bubbles* (ed. Evanoff et al.), Oxford University Press).

goods and services depends only on technology, preferences and endowments of factors of production; that aggregate supply is in turn what determines output and employment; and that while aggregate demand may depend on monetary and financial influences, demand matters only insofar as it plays a role in determining prices.

Everyone understands, of course, that we buy goods and services in exchange not for one another but for either government-issued currency or bank-issued claims on currency, and, furthermore, that we often borrow the currency or bank claims that we spend. Under some conditions these arrangements would not matter. Most economists recognize, however, that the economy in which we live does not satisfy those conditions, and hence the model under which aggregate supply, and therefore output and employment, depend only on technology, preferences and endowments, with no role for aggregate demand (or, hence, for financial influences) to affect anything other than prices and inflation, is a fiction. But we often treat it as a useful fiction nonetheless—a base case from which to begin our analysis, whether for the purposes of research, policymaking or teaching.

Unfortunately, it turns out that moving past that base case is difficult to do in a rigorous way. And confronted with the choice between theoretical rigour and accuracy of insight, macroeconomists often opt for the former. As a result, the models underlying our policy analysis often lack the basis for addressing financially driven events such as those that took place in 2007–9 and what has followed thereafter, and students of the subject mostly come away with no way whatever to understand these developments.

THE FAILURE OF RATIONALITY

In parallel, the 2007–9 crisis should make economists more willing to question the idea that all agents in the economy know (or act as if they know) both the structure of the model that governs relevant outcomes and also the distributions of the underlying random variables—in other words, the standard 'rational expectations' assumption that for some decades has anchored not only macroeconomics but also most academic research and teaching in finance. Although economists have long been aware of evidence, in part from psychology and other fields, that contradicts rational expectations (hence the burgeoning field of 'behavioural finance'), the working convention has nonetheless been to maintain the assumption that whatever departures exist do not matter for macroeconomic outcomes. But the 2007–9 crisis plainly had macroeconomic consequences.

And although it is too soon to evaluate the evidence systematically, there has already been a steady accumulation of indications that during the run-up to the crisis many key market participants—including not just individuals of modest wealth acting on their own account but also highly paid professionals working at major financial institutions—did not understand the risks they were facing. The evaluations that the major US credit rating agencies applied to securities backed by home mortgages—subprime mortgages in particular and especially those issued in 2006 and 2007—were strikingly at variance with the subsequent default experience of the underlying loans. Many forms of derivative contracts priced against these and similar securities also appear, in retrospect, to have been widely mispriced. Household-name financial institutions misjudged, in some cases by orders of magnitude, their exposure to losses on their portfolios. The question at issue here is not what was, or should have been, the market's best estimate of any given future outcome; it is the assessment, and hence the pricing, of the risk associated with those outcomes. Both in the United States and elsewhere, it was often the largest firms—the ones whose managers and employees should in principle have been most likely to think and behave as the rational expectations assumption indicates—that made the biggest mistakes.

It is possible that the decline in US house prices and the consequent sequence of events that precipitated the crisis simply constituted an extraordinary event that could not, and therefore should not, have been factored into the risk structure that market participants saw themselves facing: a proverbial 'six-sigma', or perhaps even 'ten-sigma', event. But the history of financial crises that have occurred just within recent decades has thrown up too many supposed six-sigma (or ten-sigma) events to be credible. Many people made the same claim when Long Term Capital Management had to be rescued in 1998, in the midst of the 'Asian financial crisis' and the turmoil surrounding Russia's debt obligations. Before that, the same notion emerged after a series of problems involving real estate and leveraged buyout transactions impaired many of the world's largest banks in the late 1980s and early 1990s, and, earlier still, also in the Latin American debt crisis of the early 1980s. When six-sigma events occur with this frequency, they are not six-sigma events.

For at least two reasons, the economics profession, especially including macroeconomists, has been highly reluctant to abandon the rational expectations assumption. First, doing so would be deeply subversive of the all-important role of markets in allocating the economy's scarce resources, including in particular the role of financial markets in allocating capital investment. Mispricing of assets and subsequent losses for their holders matter in themselves, as the 2007–9 crisis dramatically demonstrated, but they are also, and more fundamentally, the financial reflection of an underlying misallocation of real resources: hence too many houses (many now empty) were built in the last expansion and too many miles of fibre-optic cable (much of it never lit) were laid in the previous one. Second, the rational expectations assumption provides an analytically useful way of disciplining analysis in which forward-looking behaviour is of the essence—as is inevitably so not only in speculative securities markets but in many macroeconomic contexts too—and there is today no ready alternative to provide a comparable discipline. But to the extent that the failure of market participants to understand the risks they faced, either personally or on behalf of the financial institutions for which they worked, was central to what happened in the crisis, economic thinking grounded on the rational expectations assumption is unlikely to get to the heart of the matter.

THE ROLE OF CREDIT

A third way in which the 2007–9 crisis should make macroeconomists in particular rethink how they analyse the world is that while the crisis clearly reminded us that what happens in the financial arena matters for real economic outcomes, it also demonstrated that within the financial sphere what primarily matters for this purpose is not money but credit: what households and firms borrow, not the deposits they hold. Indeed, with the benefit of hindsight, the economics profession's half-century-long fixation with money—how to measure it, how to control it, why people hold it, and other parallel questions—now stands as a tragic distraction. In most of the economies that suffered record or near-record declines in real activity during the 2007–9 crisis, there was no significant decline in standard deposit-money aggregates. The central bank did not allow the monetary base to contract. Neither households nor firms were visibly affected by the declining real value of their monetary balances. The central bank did not restrict the supply of reserves to the banking system in a way that led to upward pressure on interest rates. Instead, the crisis demonstrated the dependence of aggregate demand, and therefore output and employment, on the volume, the availability and the price of credit, as well as on changes in the prices of non-money assets. It was borrowing, and the ability to borrow, that mattered, not deposit holding.

In some simple representations of the economy, money and credit are the same thing, or at least they co-vary identically. For example, in many familiar textbook models of the banking system, banks' assets consist of loans and reserves, the liability side of each bank's balance sheet consists of deposits and its capital, and both aggregate reserves and aggregate bank capital are fixed (by the central bank and by accumulated past profits and losses, respectively). In such models, money and credit move together identically. But in the world in which we live, depository institutions have ways of funding loans other than issuing money; their capital is not fixed (recall what happened to the capital of many banks during the crisis, once they started booking losses); banks' ability to lend depends not only on their reserves but also their capital, and often the constraint that is binding is the one on capital (as it is today, both in Europe and in the United States); and much of the lending that supports the economy's demand for goods and services is done by institutions that are not depository institutions and therefore do not hold reserves at the central bank anyway. In today's credit markets, many non-bank lenders even do the kind of 'relationship lending' that, according to the textbooks, is the special province of banks.

Adequately capturing these relationships between assets and liabilities (for both financial institutions and non-bank borrowers, and between the balance sheets of both and the spending done by household and firms) is difficult and complex. But in the wake of the 2007–9 crisis, simply carrying on with the usual money-centred models is increasingly untenable. The most obvious case in point is the huge increase in central bank liabilities implemented as part of the easier monetary policy put in place in most of the major economies, first during and then following the crisis. The Federal Reserve System, the Bank of England and the Bank of Japan have all approximately tripled the size of their balance sheets compared with the levels immediately before the crisis. Even the European Central Bank increased its balance sheet by approximately 50%. Moreover, these massive increases in monetary base have now been in place, or at least in progress, for going on half a decade. Yet in none of these economies has any corresponding pick-up in price inflation yet appeared. Especially in light of how least-squares estimation overweights outlier observations, for the next generation economists will be unable to run regressions with the price level or inflation on the left and the quantity or growth rate of central bank liabilities on the right and find any economically meaningful relationship. Policymakers should not have to use, and students should not have to learn, models that the data so plainly fail to support.

127

The Fact of Lending Institutions

A fourth way in which macroeconomics needs to adapt to what happened during the crisis is to take more explicit account of the fact that most of what households and firms borrow comes from lending institutions, rather than from individuals lending directly. What determines an institution's willingness or ability to lend? Like that of an individual, a financial institution's behaviour exhibits profit motives, risk preferences, diversification objectives and balance sheet constraints. Unlike individuals, however, institutions face capital requirements, and are therefore subject to the influence of accounting rules. In the years leading up to the 2007-9 crisis, many financial institutions took on unusually large leverage and therefore rendered themselves highly vulnerable when they began to incur losses. Many effectively took on even more leverage than their official accounts showed by assuming responsibility for assets that they were able, under the prevailing accounting rules, to keep off their balance sheets—and therefore against which they held no capital whatsoever.

Financial institutions, again unlike individuals, also face a wide variety of other regulatory constraints, some of which expand their capabilities instead of limiting them (the most obvious examples are deposit insurance and other forms of government guarantees of their liabilities). Most modern financial institutions also operate subject to limited liability (they are corporations), and they need to raise their own capital in competitive securities markets. What ends up being at risk when financial institutions lend is therefore what Louis Brandeis, in the title of his 1914 book, famously referred to as 'other people's money'. For all of these reasons, financial institutions face different incentives from those that would motivate individual lenders. It is hardly surprising that their behaviour as lenders is different too.

Furthermore, most of these institutions, at least when scaled by their volume of lending, are large and complex, and professionally managed. The resulting conflict of interest between principals (a firm's owners) and their agents (the hired managers) therefore adds to the distortions created by limited liability for the firm's losses. The incentives that motivate the actual decision makers at these lending institutions are not the same as the incentives that would govern decisions by the firms' shareholders were they to run the firm themselves. This difference in incentives between managers and shareholders compounds the difference in incentives between shareholders and the firm's debt holders: as the 2007-9 crisis showed, in one financial institution after another, the managers who made the decisions were able to do well for themselves even while the firm's shareholders lost much of their investment and, in a few cases, the debt holders lost as well. (If it had not been for government intervention, debt holders would have faced much greater losses.)

These aspects of the institutional nature of debt markets also help explain why market self-regulation carried out by debt holders and potential debt holders—to which some people had looked to take the place of supervision and regulation by agencies of the state—so obviously failed. (Unfortunately, some individuals who held this view also occupied positions of major public responsibility.) But they also have implications for the working of these markets at the macroeconomic level, and for the influence that what happens in these markets exerts on aggregate-level economic activity.

FRICTIONS AND DISTRIBUTION

Finally, the 2007–9 crisis has highlighted the shortcomings of current macroeconomic theorizing in two other ways. It has reminded us that the difficulties of shifting from one set of arrangements to another—whether those arrangements are personal, institutional or governmental—are much more important than we normally acknowledge in our models or our teaching. And it has shown that just who is affected and how, within the usual aggregates, matters importantly too.

The decline in total output that the crisis triggered is a useful illustration. In the United States, for example, the peak-to-trough decline in gross domestic product (from autumn 2007 to spring 2009) was 5.1%: a record decline for the post-Second World War period. Even so, in light of the widespread and intense public reaction (which is continuing at the time of writing), one might ask why it was such a tragedy that the nation went back to the gross domestic product it had had in mid 2005. Was the US standard of living so horribly meagre then? Were Americans mostly poverty stricken before the downturn that the financial crisis triggered? Of course not.

There are two interconnected reasons why this 5% decline in total economic output was so troubling.

First, we all make arrangements in our daily lives—where we live, what car we drive, where we send our children to school, and so on—that are very difficult for most people to alter or undo once they are in place. Most people face the same issue in their role as suppliers of labour. *Ex ante*, most people could earn their livelihoods from any of a variety of kinds of work and, for each kind, at any of many competing firms. *Ex post*, most people complete some form of education, they receive further training while at work that is specific to either their profession or their firm or both, and over time they form personal attachments to the firm for which they work and to the colleagues with whom they work. Furthermore, the arrangements that people make as consumers are frequently intertwined with their arrangements as workers. Taking a different job often implies a geographical move as well. The familiar macroeconomic aggregates over-look any such considerations. For much the same reason, in today's stan-dard macroeconomic models there is no involuntary unemployment.

Second, the impact of economic fluctuations on individuals is usually highly uneven, on both the way up and the way down; and arranging for the winners to compensate the losers is just as difficult in the macro-economic context as it is in the standard free-trade example. The reason protectionism is often so appealing in many industrialized countries is that the winners from free trade are many and widely diffused—everyone who gets to buy cheaper goods made abroad—while the losers are fewer but easy to identify and far more sharply affected: usually workers in specific manufacturing industries. Because free trade under most condi-tions makes the economy in aggregate better off, in principle the winners could compensate the losers and still come out ahead. In most countries, however, this rarely happens. From the perspective of the more general implication for economics, a finding that a particular change represents a Pareto improvement, because the winners could compensate the losers and still be better off, is of limited meaning when everyone knows that such compensation cannot, or at least will not, take place.

It is no accident that macroeconomics has mostly ignored frictions and distributional considerations, especially in recent decades. Until the 2007–9 crisis, fluctuations in output had been mostly well contained, and unemployment modest, especially compared with the events of the 1930s that gave birth to macroeconomics as a recognizable field. But in many countries the decline in economic activity that the crisis brought about was both larger and longer lasting than in most recessions since the Second World War, and the resulting unemployment was more persis-tent. With the real costs of economic downturns now more apparent than they have been in some time, it becomes more incumbent on economists to incorporate the awkward presence of both frictions and distribution effects into the constructs that they offer to policymakers and into what they teach students of the discipline.

James Tobin frequently observed that there are worse things than 3% inflation and from time to time we experience them. We just did. The reasons lie mostly outside the scope of the macroeconomic thinking of recent decades:

- the influence of financial phenomena on non-financial economic activity;
- the failure of rationality (in the standard sense) of expectations, not just idiosyncratically in isolated cases but on the part of the dominant set of financial market participants;
- within the financial–non-financial nexus, the specific importance of credit;
- the parallel fact that in the modern economy most of the lending is done by institutions; and
- the role of frictions and matters of distribution.

These features of the economy in which we live, as opposed to some simpler alternative that we can readily imagine and more easily model, are also central to the question of how policy can best respond to such events once they occur, as well as to the design of policy regimes that might render them less likely. And, in our role as educators, incorporating these ideas into what we teach our students would better equip them to understand both the economy and economic policy, not to mention enabling them to become better economists themselves if that is the path they choose.

Old Wine, New Bottles

By Andrew Haldane

The roll-call of failure from the financial crisis is long and illustrious: banks, non-banks, rating agencies, academics and regulators, to name but five. Yet the error in each case appears to have had a common cause. At root, the financial crisis was an analytical failure, an intellectual virus. This virus had contaminated almost everyone by 2007, causing them to view the pre-crisis world through spectacles far rosier than subsequent events have shown was justified.

Correctly diagnosing this intellectual virus—its genetic make-up and symptoms—is central to devising effective remedial medicine. Here, I highlight two of the dominant strains.

The first is an old virus—one as familiar as the common cold. Cycles in money and bank credit are familiar from centuries past. And yet, for perhaps a generation, the symptoms of this old virus were left untreated. That neglect allowed the infection to spread with near-fatal consequences for the financial system.

The second is a new, more virulent, strain driven by increased integration of capital markets. In the best of times, integration serves as an effective shock absorber; in the worst, as a shock-transmitter. In a tightly woven financial web, the contagious consequences of a default, such as that of Lehman Brothers, can bring the world to its knees. It is for this reason we have suffered the first genuinely global crisis in financial history. It is why this time *was* different (Reinhart and Rogoff 2009).

Having diagnosed the two strains of this virus, I highlight some of the important implications they carry for future theory and policy. Economists were clearly part of the crisis problem. We are therefore duty-bound to be part of the solution.

MONEY AND CREDIT CYCLES

As David Graeber's recent book makes clear, the world has 5,000 years of experience in managing the consequences of swings in credit and debt

(Graeber 2011). Charles Kindleberger's classic account of financial panics, manias and crashes provides a compelling narrative of the past few centuries (Kindleberger 1978). One clear, and common, history lesson emerges: debt really matters, not only to creditors and debtors but to the economy and society as a whole.

Central banks were developed, in part, as a response to that fact (Goodhart 1988). The interplay of bank money and credit and the wider economy has been pivotal to the mandate of central banks for centuries. For almost the whole of the Bank of England's 318-year history, management of central bank and commercial bank balance sheets has been one and the same: the two have been joined at the hip.

For at least a century, that has been recognized in the design of public policy frameworks. No one reading the Macmillan Report of 1931 and the Radcliffe Report of 1959 could fail to notice their similarities. For both, the management of bank money and credit was a clear public policy priority: a prerequisite for maintaining broader macroeconomic and social stability.

That orthodoxy shaped the design of policy frameworks from the interwar period onwards. Throughout this period, although the precise instruments changed, management of commercial bank balance sheets was a common policy denominator. That was true both during the immediate post-war period of financial repression and the subsequent period of financial liberalization from the early 1970s onwards (Goodhart 1988). Indeed, for much of this time no sharp distinction was made between monetary and financial stability. These were simply two sides of a coin— a coin whose common currency was bank money and credit.

The 1990s saw this orthodoxy beginning to shift. Two developments— one academic, one policy—appear to have been responsible. The first was the emergence of micro-founded dynamic stochastic general equilibrium (DSGE) models within the economics profession (Clarida *et al.* 1999; Goodfriend and King 1997). Because these models were built on real business cycle foundations, financial factors (asset prices, money and credit) played distinctly second fiddle.

These models defined a clear role for monetary policy, operating through short-term interest rates. But financial balance sheets were typically passive and endogenous: the tail to the real business cycle dog. Monetary and financial stability were separable. Indeed in these settings, activist financial stability policy was often neutral, perhaps even unhelpful. And, at least within the DSGE framework, any neglect of money and credit was likely to be benign.

At a roughly similar time, whether by coincidence or design, monetary policy frameworks were emerging that explicitly targeted inflation, rather than intermediate variables such as commercial bank money or credit (King 1997; Bernanke and Mishkin 1997). Financial factors were relegated to one among many potential information variables entering the inflation-targeting reaction function (Bernanke and Gertler 2001). These monetary policy rules, simulated through workhorse DSGE models, scarcely gave money, credit and asset prices a walk-on role (Woodford 2003).

Whether by coincidence or causality, what happened next was extraordinary. Commercial bank balance sheets grew by the largest amount in human history. For example, bank assets in the United Kingdom were around half of annual gross domestic product for around a century from 1880 to 1970 (Haldane 2011). In the following thirty-five years, bank assets rose by an order of magnitude to more than 500% of gross domestic product. A similar pattern was found across banking systems in the other advanced economies.

This balance sheet explosion was, in a sense, no one's fault and no one's responsibility. Not banks, which were harvesting handsome profits and being offered financing at close to risk-free rates. Not monetary policy authorities, whose focus was primarily inflation and whose models scarcely permitted bank balance sheets a role. And not financial regulators, whose focus was the strength of individual financial institutions and whose models suggested risk had been scattered to the four winds.

Yet this policy neglect, contrary to much pre-crisis thinking, has since shown itself to be far from benign. The collapse of overinflated bank balance sheets was the catalyst for the global financial crisis, requiring huge injections of external capital and liquidity into banks, often backed by government. Having been in the fast lane for twenty years, global credit growth has gone into reverse gear, starving households and companies of necessary funds and acting as a drag on the world economy. Five years on, this retrenchment shows no sign of abating.

None of this should have come as a surprise. For at least the past 150 years, the cycle in credit has been every bit as regular as the cycle in output (Schularick and Taylor 2012; Aikman *et al.* 2010). But its effects are, if anything, even more damaging. Credit cycles have a duration and amplitude that is roughly double that of the business cycle. And when credit booms turn to bust, the result is typically a far deeper and longer than average recession (Schularick and Taylor 2012). Like Macmillan in the 1930s and Radcliffe in the 1950s, financial history should have caused us to take credit cycles seriously.

This old lesson, relearned over the past few years, carries important implications for the economics profession and the execution of public policy. For the economics profession it underscores the importance of subdisciplines such as economic and financial history, money, banking and finance and the interplay between economic and financial systems. All three were crucial ingredients in the crisis and yet all three fell out of fashion during the pre-crisis boom. Their disappearance from the core curriculum made a significant contribution to their neglect in policy-making. This error now needs to be corrected.

The single most important lesson for public policy is that leaning against the cycle in credit is as essential a prerequisite of stability in the real economy as low inflation. This lesson is increasingly being heeded internationally. Today, it goes by the name macroprudential policy, to distinguish it from the prudential oversight of individual financial firms (Crockett 2000). Recently, a number of countries have set up agencies with an explicitly macroprudential mandate.

For example, in the United Kingdom a new Financial Policy Committee, housed in the Bank of England, charged with this task was set up in 2011 (see HM Treasury 2012). The Financial Policy Committee will have the tools of the trade necessary to calm, if not completely tame, the credit cycle. Like the Monetary Policy Committee, it will aim to smooth out credit peaks and troughs symmetrically to support the resilience of the financial system. This institutional arrangement aims to guard against a future episode of malign balance sheet neglect.

NETWORKS AND EXPECTATIONS

The social dynamics during the Arab Spring in many ways closely resembled financial system dynamics following the failure of Lehman Brothers in 2008: sharp discontinuities driven by fear and uncertainty. This was no coincidence. Both are complex, adaptive systems. When stressed, these systems are known to behave in a non-linear, unpredictable fashion due to cascading actions and reactions among agents. These systems exhibit a robust-yet-fragile property: swan-like serenity one minute, riot-like calamity the next (Watts 2002; Haldane 2009).

These dynamics do not emerge from most mainstream models of the financial system or real economy. The reason for this is simple: the majority of these mainstream models use the framework of a single representative agent (or a small number of them) (Kirman 2010). That effectively neuters the possibility of complex interactions between agents shaping system dynamics. It is precisely these interactions that held the key to explaining the discontinuities of the financial crisis and the Arab Spring.

The perils of the representative agent framework for understanding financial system dynamics were brilliantly demonstrated by Martin Hellwig well before the crisis began (Hellwig 1995). Imagine a set of 100 banks. Bank 1 uses sight deposits of $100 to lend for one month to Bank 2. Bank 2 in turn on-lends to Bank 3 for two months, and so on up to Bank 100. This is a classic credit intermediation chain. And on the face of it, this chain appears relatively robust: each representative bank is running a maturity mismatch of only one month and, on average, has net debt of only $1.

Yet, in reality, this financial system is inherently fragile, a fragility completely obscured by looking through the lens of the representative bank. In the example, the financial system as a whole is running a maturity mismatch of $n - 1$ (or 99) months. The financial system contains gross debt of $(n - 1) \times \$100$: $9,900. It is these gross, system-wide properties that matter for behavioural dynamics and stability.

To see this, imagine concerns arise over Bank 1 and its depositors run. This run is in danger of cascading through the entire network, as firms along the chain seek to cover their maturing liabilities by foreclosing on their assets (which are loans to other banks), all the way to Bank 100. The system-wide maturity mismatch potentially then causes collapse of the entire credit chain (Gai *et al.* 2011). The same dynamics may arise in reverse at the other end of the chain. If Bank 100 defaults, credit problems may then cascade down the chain all the way to Bank 1. Gross intra-financial system debt risks system-wide bankruptcy.

Neither of these examples is especially far-fetched as a description of the pre-crisis financial system. In the early years of this century, financial chains lengthened dramatically, system-wide maturity mismatches widened alarmingly and intra-financial system claims ballooned exponentially—all three of the ingredients in the stylized example (Brunnermeier and Oehmke 2010). The system became, in consequence, a hostage to its weakest link. When that broke, so too did the system as a whole.

These network links were not just financial. Higher-order network links give rise to destabilizing dynamics in expectations (Morris and Shin 2008). Every bank in a financial chain or network is potentially exposed to every other at some degree of separation. In a complex web, what matters is not just your counterparty, but your counterparty's counterparty's counterparty. Because those links are impossible to monitor, fears about failure may quickly destabilize the whole web. Any bad apple, real or imagined,

137

can contaminate the whole barrel. Higher-order networks generate not so much risk as uncertainty (Caballero and Krishnamurthy 2008).

That, too, was the Lehman Brothers story. It was network uncertainty, rather than risk, that caused the freeze in financial markets. But this deep freeze extended well beyond financial borders. Communications networks and social media propagated fear globally. That is why the backdraft from the failure of Lehman Brothers was felt as severely in New Delhi as it was in New York. That is why the real economy experienced a cliff edge every bit as precipitous as the financial system. And that is why the world experienced its first ever truly global crisis.

Then, adverse expectational dynamics, in a networked world, drove us to a new economic and financial equilibrium. Those same dynamics explain why the Arab Spring sprang and spread, as social media propagated (now-positive) expectational contagion. They explain why people were rioting on the streets of London in 2011. And they explain why the bond market continues to drive the Eurozone into endless self-fulfilling bouts of instability.

Conventional models, based on the representative agent and with expectations mimicking fundamentals, have no hope of capturing these system dynamics. They are fundamentally ill suited to capturing today's networked world, in which social media shape expectations, shape behaviour, shape outcomes. This is true irrespective of the socioeconomic system under study.

These network dynamics carry important, and new, implications for the economics profession and for public policy. For economics, they suggest that investment needs to be made in a new mainstream set of models: ones in which complexity and higher-order agent interactions are taken seriously. The construction and simulation of highly non-linear dynamics in systems of multiple equilibria represent unfamiliar territory for most in the economics profession. They will call for a human capital investment every bit as great as the one that economists have made in DSGE models over the past twenty years.

The cupboard is not bare. Many of the models and techniques necessary for understanding these systems have been developed by sociologists, physicists, ecologists, epidemeologists and anthropologists, among others. Economists are now beginning to take up the baton (see, for example, Haldane and May 2011). This is not a journey into the unknown. It will, however, require a sense of academic adventure that was sadly absent in the pre-crisis period.

For public policy, the experience of having to repair the financial web is leading to a gradual, if discernible, rethink of regulatory orthodoxy. New data on this web will be crucial if network uncertainties (as distinct from risks) are to be adequately understood and priced by regulators and market participants. Policymakers should aspire to the sort of maps that are commonplace among meteorologists, with real-time visualizations of the contours of risk to allow remedial action (Ali *et al.* 2012).

It may also mean a rethink of appropriate control tools. Historically, finance has sought to regulate financial behaviour. In a densely interwoven web, it may make more sense to regulate financial structure instead. Post-crisis efforts to reconfigure the structure of banking (such as the Volcker rule in the United States and the Vickers proposals in the United Kingdom) and the topology of trading (such as the introduction of central counterparties) suggest some swing has already begun in this direction.

Finally, real-time interactions in a complex social web may call for a rethink of policy communication. Harnessing rapidly adapting expectations has never been more important. Social media and modern communications have hastened the spread of panic, fear and exuberance. And, contrary to efficient markets theory, these hopes and fears may themselves be driving fundamentals rather than vice versa (Akerlof and Shiller 2009). Public policymakers, responding to events ranging from the Arab Spring to the Eurozone crisis, are struggling to adapt to this new world.

CONCLUSION

Let me conclude with two speculative thoughts: the first for academic economists and the second for policymaking economists.

Academia keeps score in ways that look increasingly antiquated. Journal publication remains the main currency, but it is a devalued currency, at least as a medium of exchange for ideas. Some of the top names in the economics world have taken to social media and the blogosphere to propagate their ideas. This has the benefit not just of immediacy but reach. It amounts to using those network externalities to academic advantage.

For policymakers, it is difficult to think of a more challenging environment in the post-war period. The macroeconomy is well outside the corridor of self-stabilizing dynamics described so beautifully by Axel Leijonhufvud in the 1960s (Leijonhufvud 1968). Ideally, public policy would step into this breach, restoring confidence about the future. But policymakers face the self-same uncertainty. They too are operating in uncharted territory, outside of the corridor.

In such an uncertain environment, what can policy do? Communication and adaptation will be key. Communication to keep in check expectations if they risk becoming destabilizing by panic or fear. Adaptation to flex policy in response to changed circumstances, experience and expectations. And, perhaps most important of all, communication about adaptation in the policy framework, explaining why change is needed.

Monetary policy experience is salutary. From the end of the Second World War adaptations of monetary frameworks came thick and fast. These changes eroded policy credibility, for change was typically taken to mean failure. In fact, monetary policymakers were in a period of intense learning. Today, policymakers are having to learn more intensively than they needed to during that earlier period. It is therefore crucial that adaptations to today's policy frameworks are interpreted not as failure, but as necessary steps towards success.

REFERENCES

Aikman, D., A. G. Haldane and B. Nelson. 2010. Curbing the credit cycle. Speech (available at www.bankofengland.co.uk/publications/pages/speeches/2010/463.aspx).

Akerlof, G. A., and R. J. Shiller. 2009. *Animal Spirits: How Human Psychology Drives the Economy, and Why It Matters for Global Capitalism.* Princeton University Press.

Ali, R., A. G. Haldane and P. Nahai-Williamson. 2012. Towards a common financial language. Speech (available at www.bankofengland.co.uk/publications/Documents/speeches/2012/speech552.pdf).

Bernanke, B. and M. Gertler. 2001. Should central banks respond to movements in asset prices? *American Economic Review* 91(2):253–257.

Bernanke, B., and F. Mishkin. 1997. Inflation targeting: a new framework for monetary policy? *Journal of Economic Perspectives* 11(2):97–116.

Brunnermeier, M. K., and M. Oehmke. 2010. The maturity rat race. NBER Working Paper 16607.

Caballero, R. J., and A. Krishnamurthy. 2008. Collective risk management in a flight to quality episode. *Journal of Finance* 63(5):2195–2230.

Clarida, R., J. Galí and M. Gertler. 1999. The science of monetary policy: a New Keynesian perspective. *Journal of Economic Literature* 37(4):1661–1707.

Crockett, A. D. 2000. In search of anchors for financial and monetary stability. Speech at the SUERF Colloquium in Vienna (27–29 April; available at www.bis.org/speeches/sp000427.htm).

Gai, P., A. Haldane and S. Kapadia. 2011. Complexity, concentration and contagion. *Journal of Monetary Economics* 58(5):453–470.

Goodfriend, M., and R. G. King. 1997. The new neoclassical synthesis and the role of monetary policy. In *NBER Macroeconomics Annual 1997* (ed. B. S. Bernanke and J. J. Rotemberg), volume 12, pp. 231–296. Cambridge, MA: MIT Press.

Goodhart, C. A. E. 1988. *The Evolution of Central Banks*. Cambridge, MA: MIT Press.

Graeber, D. 2011. *Debt: The First 5,000 Years*. New York: Melville House.

Haldane, A. G. 2009. Rethinking the financial network. Speech (available at www.bankofengland.co.uk/publications/Documents/speeches/2009/speech386.pdf).

Haldane, A. G. 2011. Control rights (and wrongs). Speech (available at www.bankofengland.co.uk/publications/Documents/speeches/2011/speech525.pdf).

Haldane, A. G., and R. M. May. 2011. Systemic risk in banking ecosystems. *Nature* 469:351–355.

Hellwig, M. 1995. Systemic aspects of risk management in banking and finance. *Swiss Journal of Economics and Statistics* 131(4/2):723–737.

HM Treasury. 2012. A new approach to financial regulation: secured stability, protecting consumers. Policy document (available at www.hm-treasury.gov.uk/d/fin_fs_bill_policy_document_jan2012.pdf).

Kindleberger, C. 1978. *Manias, Panics and Crashes—A History of Financial Crises*. Wiley

King, M. 1997. Changes in UK monetary policy: rules and discretion in practice. *Journal of Monetary Economics* 39:81–97.

Kirman, A. 2010. *Complex Economics: Individual and Collective Rationality*. London: Routledge.

Leijonhufvud, A. 1968. *On Keynesian Economics and the Economics of Keynes: A Study in Monetary Theory*. Oxford University Press.

Macmillan Committee Report. 1931. *Report of the Committee on Finance and Industry*. Command 3897. London: HMSO.

Morris, S., and H. S. Shin. 2008. Financial regulation in a system context. *Brookings Papers on Economic Activity* 39(2):229–274.

Radcliffe Committee Report. 1959. *Report of the Committee on the Working of the Monetary System*. Command 827. London: HMSO.

Reinhart, C. M., and K. S. Rogoff. 2009. *This Time Is Different: Eight Centuries of Financial Folly*. Princeton University Press.

Schularick, M., and A. M. Taylor. 2012. Credit booms gone bust: monetary policy, leverage cycles, and financial crises, 1870–2008. *American Economic Review* 102(2):1029–1061.

Watts, D. J. 2002. A simple model of global cascades on random networks. *Proceedings of the National Academy of Sciences of the USA* 99(9):5766–5771.

Woodford, M. 2003. *Interest and Prices: Foundations of a Theory of Monetary Policy*. Princeton University Press.

141

Back to the Drawing Board for Macroeconomics

By Paul Ormerod and Dirk Helbing

INTRODUCTION AND BACKGROUND

In November 2010, Jean-Claude Trichet, then governor of the European Central Bank, opened the Bank's flagship annual Central Banking Conference. He challenged the scientific community to develop radically new approaches to understanding the economy:

> When the crisis came, the serious limitations of existing economic and financial models immediately became apparent. Macro models failed to predict the crisis and seemed incapable of explaining what was happening to the economy in a convincing manner. As a policymaker during the crisis, I found the available models of limited help. In fact, I would go further: in the face of the crisis, we felt abandoned by conventional tools.

Trichet went on to say:

> We need to develop complementary tools to improve the robustness of our overall framework. In this context, I would very much welcome inspiration from other disciplines: physics, engineering, psychology, biology. Bringing experts from these fields together with economists and central bankers is potentially very creative and valuable. Scientists have developed sophisticated tools for analysing complex dynamic systems in a rigorous way. These models have proved helpful in understanding many important but complex phenomena: epidemics, weather patterns, crowd psychology, magnetic fields.

It is instructive, in the light of this, to consider how the US authorities reacted to the financial crisis after the collapse of Lehman Brothers in September 2008. During the Great Depression of the 1930s, the cumulative fall in real gross domestic product was some 27%. The previous peak

143

level of output, in 1929, was not regained until 1939, a whole decade later. The recent recession has been the most serious in peacetime for all Western economies since the second half of the nineteenth century (Ormerod 2010a). So far, the falls in output since 2008 that have come about as a result of the financial crisis have been less devastating. In the United States, output fell some 3% and has already risen above its previous peak level. In the major European economies, gross domestic product fell by around 6%. The strength of the recovery in these countries has not generally been as strong as the recovery in the United States, but even so the experience has been markedly better than it was in the 1930s.

However, during the current financial crisis, the authorities did not make use of the dominant intellectual concept in academic macroeconomics of the last thirty years. This concept started off as real business cycle theory (Kydland and Prescott 1982), and was then developed into dynamic stochastic general equilibrium (DSGE) theory. (For a description of the scientific state of the art when the financial crisis began, see, for example, Tovar (2009).)

Fortunately—and this illustrates the role of chance and contingency in human affairs—Ben Bernanke, governor of the Federal Reserve, was an expert not in DSGE models but in the economic history of the Great Depression itself. He and his colleagues operated under conditions of great uncertainty, and essentially they tried to avoid the key mistakes made during the early 1930s in the United States. They maintained an expansionary monetary policy, in contrast to the contractions of the Great Depression, and defended the banks. As previously described (Ormerod 2010b), in the crucial days following the collapse of Lehman Brothers, they took a number of purely administrative measures.

- They nationalized the main mortgage companies, Fannie Mae and Freddie Mac.
- They effectively nationalized the giant insurance company AIG.
- They eliminated investment banks.
- They forced mergers of giant retail banks.
- They guaranteed money-market funds.

This last action, although it has received little publicity, was possibly the single most important act carried out by the authorities, averting an immediate and catastrophic liquidity crisis. Its impact was probably even greater than that of the $700 billion Troubled Asset Relief Programme, which was played out in the full light of the democratic spotlight.

One immediate implication of the above is the pressing need to reintroduce economic history into the teaching of economics at all levels. Although the world has seen many financial crises in its history (Reinhart and Rogoff 2009), there have been only two such global crises over the past century: in the early 1930s and the late 2000s. The Maddison database (Maddison 1995) of seventeen leading Western economies contains annual data on real gross domestic product going back to 1870. The only years when almost all these countries were simultaneously in recession (that is, when the growth in real gross domestic product was less than zero) were 1930–32 and 2009.

As noted above, an awareness of economic history rather than of DSGE models enabled the authorities to muddle through the latest crisis. Even after all this time economists have not arrived at a consensus on the precise cause of the Great Depression, but our knowledge about it is not zero.

All students of economics would benefit from studying certain key episodes in economic history. In addition to the Great Depression, the oil shock crisis of the 1970s and the contrasting transitions to peacetime after the two world wars are examples that spring readily to mind. The period after the First World War was characterized by deep recessions in some countries. Serious problems with both international trade and the world monetary system persisted throughout the interwar period. In contrast, output after the Second World War recovered very rapidly, even in the defeated countries, and a long period of unparalleled growth followed. During this period, inflation rates in the West were close to each other. However, in the mid 1970s there was a rapid and dramatic widening of the differences between them. In 1975, for example, the inflation rate in Germany was only 4%, but it was above 20% in both Italy and the United Kingdom. The analysis of such formative periods raises many important questions in economic theory.

With this general background comment in mind, the second section of this chapter briefly considers existing theory in macroeconomics, and specifically theories of the business cycle. The third section sets out what we regard as the key intellectual concepts that are needed to rebuild macroeconomics. The final section offers a conclusion.

BUSINESS CYCLE THEORY

There are two features that distinguish capitalism from all previously existing forms of social and economic organization. First, there is slow but steady real economic growth over time. Second, there are persistent fluctuations around the underlying rate of expansion. It is not our concern in this paper to discuss theories of economic growth except to note that economics does not really have a satisfactory theory to explain this phenomenon. Our focus is instead on the fluctuations in growth: so-called business cycles.

A recent theme in discussions about redesigning the teaching of macroeconomics is that of the need for students to know, in addition to economic history, the history of economic thought. Difficult problems have been addressed by great scholars in the past, and it is argued that students should be familiar with these efforts. It is hard to disagree completely with such an argument, if only because the current generation in any science, or would-be science, stands on the shoulders of the giants of the past. It would certainly be helpful for students to be aware of the work of business cycle theorists such as Marx, Keynes, Hayek and Schumpeter, all of whom can be regarded as working in theoretical frameworks in which in practice the economy spends most of its time out of equilibrium, even if an equilibrium exists in principle.

However, in our opinion too much time could be spent on the study of economic thought. Students of physics need to learn Newtonian physics at some point because of the very powerful empirical evidence that supports such theories (within the appropriate settings). However, such matching of theory with empirical evidence is very much lacking in macroeconomic theories of the business cycle.

There are several key features of real gross domestic product growth that a scientific model should be able to replicate: for example, the autocorrelation function of the time series and its Fourier transform pair, the power spectrum. Both the duration of recessions and their cumulative sizes follow highly non-Gaussian distributions, as does the time period between recessions. These are obvious examples of so-called stylized facts that a genuinely scientific model ought to be able to explain.

Macroeconomics needs to become an empirically based science that is able to explain fundamental features of the economy. A glaring example of the lack of progress made in this area is the continuing lack of consensus on the size of the fiscal multiplier: a fundamental concept in macroeconomic theory. In his *General Theory* of 1936, Keynes hazarded the opinion that for the UK economy, the eventual increase in real gross domestic product following a debt-financed expansion of public expenditure would be between two and three times the initial stimulus. However, the openness of the current UK economy (as well as of other European economies) and the associated marginal propensity to import mean that the multiplier is very unlikely to be so high. Indeed, the first systematic comparison of macroeconometric models of the United Kingdom, which was carried out over thirty years ago (Laury *et al.* 1978), obtained estimates from three different models of between 0.5 and 1.2.

Even now, there are huge differences in the literature on the estimated size of this basic macroeconomic concept. Ramey argues that the multiplier in the United States, which is of course a much more closed economy in trade terms than any individual European economy, is between 0.8 and 1.5 (Ramey 2011). However, Barro and Redlick (2011) argue that multipliers for non-defence purchases cannot even be reliably estimated at all because of a lack of suitable instruments. They conclude:

> The estimated multiplier for defense spending is 0.6–0.7 at the median unemployment rate. There is some evidence that this multiplier rises with the extent of economic slack and reaches 1.0 when the unemployment rate is around 12%. Since the defense-spending multiplier is typically less than one, greater spending tends to crowd out other components of GDP [gross domestic product].

It is not our purpose to adjudicate in any way on this debate. We simply note that, some eighty years after the concept was first developed, empirical estimates of the fiscal multiplier, a fundamental concept taught to all levels of students, vary enormously.

Of course the current dominant concept in macroeconomic theory—that of DSGE models—has an altogether different intellectual pedigree. The numerical solution of such models is itself a non-trivial task.[1] This in itself is not necessarily an objection to such models, but we note that the maximum number of agents considered in the referenced special issue was as low as ten. As the number of agents in the model grows, the dimension of the state space expands, and forming expectations entails integrating over a higher-dimensional set of shocks. This does seem to limit the degree of heterogeneity that can currently be captured by these models.

This is not the place to carry out a detailed critique of such models. It is, however, important to note one point. The intellectual pedigree of DSGE models goes back to the famous Lucas critique of macroeconometric models (Lucas 1976). Lucas argued that policy evaluation (for example,

---

[1] See, for example, the 2011 special issue of the *Journal of Economic Dynamics and Control* that was edited by R. Wouter, J. Den Haan, K. L. Judd and M. Juillard.

using the fiscal multiplier estimate as discussed earlier) in such models could be very misleading, because the parameters of such models might themselves not be invariant to the policies carried out. One of the key features of the models of the 'new macroeconomics' was held to be that the parameters that characterize the preferences of a representative agent and the production technologies of a representative firm as well as the exogenous structural shocks are policy invariant. However, Chang, Kim and Schorfheide have recently shown that this is not necessarily true (Chang *et al.* 2011).

Olivier Blanchard, chief economist at the International Monetary Fund, expressed a change of mind about such models as a result of the financial crisis. In an MIT working paper released in August 2008 (Blanchard 2008), merely weeks before the collapse of Lehman Brothers, Blanchard argued that:

> For a long while after the explosion of macroeconomics in the 1970s, the field looked like a battlefield. Over time, however, largely because facts do not go away, a largely shared vision both of fluctuations and of methodology has emerged.... The state of macro is good.

This echoed Lucas's 2003 presidential address to the American Economic Association, when he claimed that 'the central problem of depression-prevention has been solved'. Blanchard went on to say:

> DSGE models have become ubiquitous. Dozens of teams of researchers are involved in their construction. Nearly every central bank has one, or wants to have one. They are used to evaluate policy rules, to do conditional forecasting, or even sometimes to do actual forecasting.... Macro-economics is going through a period of great progress.

However, within a matter of months, Blanchard changed his opinions dramatically. In another MIT working paper, written in January 2009 (Blanchard 2009), he identified four main reasons for the crisis.

- Assets were created, sold and bought that appeared much less risky than they truly were.
- Securitization led to complex and hard-to-value assets being on the balance sheets of financial institutions.
- Securitization and globalization led to increasing connectedness between financial institutions, both within and across countries.
- Leverage increased.

We now move on to consider ways in which macroeconomics might address such issues.

REBUILDING ECONOMICS

We are not suggesting that standard economics be replaced completely. For example, the concept that agents alter their behaviour when incentives change appears to be a universal law of behaviour in the social sciences.

However, a fundamental shift in the underlying view of economics is needed. We live now in a densely networked, strongly coupled and largely interdependent world, which behaves completely differently from a system of independently optimizing decision makers. These systems often behave in a counter-intuitive way and, because of the speed of change, the ability of agents to learn is severely constrained. Networking promotes cascading effects and extreme events (see, for example, Helbing *et al.* 2005; Ormerod and Colbaugh 2006; Helbing 2010) and crises. Furthermore, strong couplings can cause systemic instabilities (See, for example, Helbing 2011; Gao *et al.* 2012).

Traditional ways of thinking about both the business cycle in general and crises in particular are essentially based on an equilibrium view of the world. In this view, the economy can certainly be out of equilibrium, and sometimes far from it. However, such behaviour essentially arises from exogenous shocks. Instead, we need to appreciate the endogenous nature of the business cycle that is inherent to the system and not generally caused by external shocks. The idea that the cycle is endogenous has a long tradition in economics, starting with Marx and including Keynes, Hayek, Schumpeter and Goodwin, for example. Modern network theory can be regarded as emerging from this tradition, rather than from what has become the dominant, equilibrium paradigm of modern economics. A detailed discussion of the vision of the economy as an evolving complex system is given in, for example, the volumes edited by Anderson *et al.* (1988), Arthur *et al.* (1997), Blume and Durlauf (2006) and Farmer *et al.* (2012).

The representative agent approach must be abandoned. For example, the representative agent model cannot describe cascading effects well. These are not determined by the *average* stability but by the *weakest* link (see, for example, Ormerod and Evans 2011). The representative agent approach also neglects effects of spatial interactions and heterogeneities in the preferences of market participants. When these are considered, the conclusions can be completely different, sometimes even opposite. For example, there may be an 'outbreak' rather than a breakdown of cooperative behaviour (see, for example, Helbing and Yu 2009).

Furthermore, the representative agent approach does not allow one to understand particular effects of the structure of interactions within the network, which may promote or obstruct cooperativeness, trust, public safety, etc. Neglecting such network effects can lead to a serious underestimation of the importance that 'social capital' has for the creation of economic value and social well-being.

Awareness among economists of the limitations of the rational agent paradigm has steadily increased. In fact, these limitations have been stressed already in the past by well-known economists. For example, Pareto said that people spent some of their time making non-rational decisions and the rest of their time rationalizing them. Keynes emphasized that 'expectations matter' and placed great importance on market psychology ('animal spirits').

In a seminal 1955 paper, Simon forcefully argued that 'economic man' is in general unable to compute optimal decisions, but instead uses 'satisficing' rules of thumb (Simon 1955). Mainstream economics has subverted Simon's revolutionary message, so that satisficing is now seen as an example of rationality. Agents search amongst alternatives until they find one that is satisfactory, judging that the time and effort involved in further search for a better one is not likely to be matched by the potential increase in benefits. However, Simon argued that in many situations, even *ex post*, the optimal decision can never be known. Tversky and Kahnemann (1974) showed in laboratory experiments that individual decisions under uncertainty are much better described by heuristics, and that these may lead to systematic biases. Schumpeter and Hayek already had a 'complexity' view of economics with competing strategies and evolutionary selection. But these ideas were largely forgotten when the rational expectations paradigm in macroeconomics spread in the 1970s and 1980s.

Therefore, it is still a key challenge in economics to develop a fundamental model of agent behaviour that is empirically grounded in twenty-first-century reality. Incentives still matter, but in addition agent behaviour in networked systems is influenced directly by the behaviour of others. Tastes and preferences are not fixed, but evolve in ways that depend upon the decisions of others. Schelling introduced one such model, the so-called binary choice with externalities (Schelling 1973). Agents face a binary choice—for example, buy or sell—and their decision can influence the decisions of others directly. More recent formulations draw on models of social learning behaviour from other social sciences such as anthropology and cultural evolution to build an empirically grounded theory of learning and adaptive behaviour for complex socioeconomic systems (see, for example, Brock and Durlauf 2001; Rendell *et al.* 2010; Bentley *et al.* 2011a,b; Hahn and Bentley 2003; Bentley and Ormerod 2011).

Macroeconomics has, in recent decades, been much less receptive than microeconomics to new ideas from other disciplines. For example, it is by now well known that one of the causes of the financial crisis was the non-Gaussian nature of the distribution of asset price changes. The fat tails of these distributions mean that large changes, although still infrequent, are many orders of magnitude more likely than is implied by the Gaussian distribution. Yet the Value at Risk models implemented in many financial institutions assumed that price changes were normally distributed. Mandelbrot had shown as early as 1963 that this was not the case. In the late 1990s, econophysicists demonstrated beyond doubt, using evidence from a very wide range of markets, that price changes were non-Gaussian (see, for example, Mantegna and Stanley 2000; Bouchaud and Potters 2003). Literally hundreds of scientific papers are published and/or presented at scientific conferences on this topic.

Furthermore, covariance matrices of financial returns are the key input parameters to Markowitz's classical portfolio selection problem (Markowitz 1952), which forms the basis of modern investment theory. For any practical use of the theory, it is therefore necessary to obtain reliable estimates for the covariance matrices of real-life financial returns. The effect of estimation noise (in the covariance matrix of financial returns) on the solution of the classical portfolio selection problem was studied extensively as long ago as the 1980s.

The problem of noise in financial covariance matrices was put in a new light by the findings of econophysicists obtained by the application of random matrix theory (see, for example, Laloux *et al.* 1999, 2000; Plerou *et al.* 1999). These studies showed that correlation matrices determined from financial return series contain such a high amount of noise that, apart from a few large eigenvalues and the corresponding eigenvectors, their structure can be regarded as random (in the example analysed by Laloux *et al.* (1999), 94% of the spectrum could be fitted by that of a purely random matrix). This not only showed that the amount of estimation noise in financial correlation matrices is large, but also provided the basis for a technique that can be used for an improved estimation of the correlations. Again, however, the findings of econophysics were ignored by mainstream economics.

The implication of the non-Gaussian statistics and the portfolio estimation noise was that assets were created, bought and sold that were actually much more risky than they appeared. The fat-tail problem meant that the probability of large price changes was drastically underestimated in the case of individual assets. And the poor empirical determination of the covariance matrix meant that the level of diversification in portfolios was thought to be considerably greater than it really was.

More generally, the authorities deluded themselves that the massive volume of debt contracts had been priced rationally and hence optimally. In the true spirit of the rational agent, rational expectations view of the world, they believed that agents had used the correct model in setting the prices, whereas of course they had not. If loans and debts had been priced rationally and optimally, the logical implication was that the interest payments receivable would exactly cover the risks involved on the loans. So, if an individual or institution defaulted on a loan, sufficient provision had been made via the optimal pricing of the loan to cover the loss arising from any such default. There was no need to tie up capital unnecessarily in liquid assets when it could be lent out at a profit. Across a portfolio of many such loans, the default of a single loan simply could not cause any problem.

In the brave new world of DSGE theory, the possibility of a systemic collapse—of a cascade of defaults across the system—was therefore never envisaged at all. Modern complexity theory, and specifically network theory, tells us that in an interconnected system the *same* initial shock would lead to dramatically different outcomes if we could replay history many times. Most of the time, shocks are contained and do not spread very far through the system. But, in principle, a shock of identical size could instead trigger a cascade of global proportions. We are in the realm of uncertainty here—finding it hard even to determine the probability distribution of expected outcomes—rather than a world of precise calculation of risk. Indeed, it may even be impossible to calculate the risk. The mean value and the standard deviation of a sample can always be calculated, but with fat tails the population mean and standard deviation may not exist at all.

We have to be very careful in drawing conclusions about the degree of connectivity and the vulnerability of a system to a global cascade following a shock. In principle, greater connectedness can strengthen a system, but given the ludicrously low liquid asset ratios with which banks were operating, it appears plausible that the opposite actually happened (Battiston *et al.* 2012).

As a final specific comment we note Blanchard's final *mea culpa* from his 2009 working paper (cited earlier): that leverage increased. Blanchard helpfully translates this phrase into English:

> Financial institutions financed their portfolios with less and less capital, thus increasing the rate of return on that capital. What were the reasons behind it? Surely, optimism, and the underestimation of risk, was again part of it.

Further comment is superfluous.

CONCLUSIONS

It is hard to escape the conclusion that mainstream macroeconomics needs to go back to the drawing board and be largely redesigned, more or less from scratch. Key aspects of the research programme to rebuild macroeconomics include the following.

- Abandon the representative agent.
- Introduce agent heterogeneity.
- Develop more realistic models of agent behavior that incorporate, for example,
  - cognitive complexity, subjectivity, emotions and learning,
  - the interaction of emotional states with belief-based processes,
  - social learning and
  - self-image.
- Recognize that the macroeconomy is a system of coupled dynamic networks.
- Build in the potential for cascades across various networks:
  - the direct financial linkages between institutions,
  - the networks across which opinions are formed in financial markets,
  - the networks across which the 'animal spirits' of commercial companies are determined, and
  - the networks across which optimism or pessimism spread amongst consumers.

Important questions to address include the following.

- What phenomena may occur in strongly coupled and interdependent systems and under what conditions? How should we characterize these phenomena? What universality classes exist?
- What are the interdependencies between structure, dynamics and function? How do networks affect the behaviour of their components? Are there properties that individual components 'inherit' from the networks they belong to?
- What are the limits of predictability and controllability in complex, networked systems? Is the economic system designed in a controllable way from a cybernetic point of view? If not, what would have to be changed to make the system more manageable?

In short, we have an agenda that is essentially focused on networks. The properties of networks in terms of their propensity to either transmit or absorb shocks, the interactions between the agents in any given network, the interactions between the emergent macro features of networks and individual agents, and the interactions between the various coupled networks that make up the economy of the twenty-first century.

REFERENCES

Anderson, P. W., K. Arrow and D. Pines. 1988. *The Economy as an Evolving Complex System.* Redwood City, CA: Addison-Wesley.

Arthur, W. B., S. N. Durlauf and D. Lane (eds). 1997. *The Economy as an Evolving Complex System II.* Santa Fe Institute Series. Boulder, CO: Westview Press.

Barro, R. J., and C. J. Redlick. 2011. Macroeconomic effects from government purchases and taxes. *Quarterly Journal of Economics* 126:51–102.

Battiston, S., D. Delli-Gatti, M. Gallegati, B. C. Greenwald and J. E. Stiglitz. 2012. Liaisons dangereuses: increasing connectivity, risk sharing, and systemic risk. *Journal of Economic Dynamics and Control,* forthcoming.

Bentley, R. A., and P. Ormerod. 2011. Agents, intelligence, and social atoms. In *Integrating Science and the Humanities* (ed. M. Collard and E. Slingerland). Oxford University Press.

Bentley, R. A., M. O'Brien and P. Ormerod. 2011a. Quality versus mere popularity: a conceptual map for understanding human behaviour. *Mind and Society* 10: 181–191.

Bentley, R. A., P. Ormerod and M. Batty. 2011b. Evolving social influence in large populations. *Behavioural Ecology and Sociobiology* 65:537–546.

Blanchard, O. J. 2008. The state of macro. MIT Department of Economics Working Paper 08-17.

Blanchard, O. J. 2009. The crisis: basic mechanism and appropriate policies. MIT Department of Economics Working Paper 09-01.

Blume, L. E., and S. N. Durlauf (eds). 2006. *The Economy as an Evolving Complex System III*. Oxford University Press.

Bouchaud, J.-P., and M. Potters. 2003. *Theory of Financial Risk and Derivative Pricing: From Statistical Physics to Risk Management*. Cambridge University Press.

Brock, W. A., and S. Durlauf. 2001. Discrete choice with social interactions. *Review of Economic Studies* 68:235–260.

Chang, Y., S.-B. Kim and F. Schorfheide. 2011. Labor-market heterogeneity, aggregation and the policy-(in)variance of DSGE model parameters. RCER Working Papers 566, University of Rochester, Rochester Center for Economic Research (RCER).

Farmer, J. D., M. Gallegati, C. Hommes, A. P. Kirman, P. Ormerod, S. Cincotti, A. Sanchez and D. Helbing. 2012. A complex systems approach to constructing better models for managing financial markets and the economy. *European Physics Journal*, forthcoming.

Gao, J., S. V. Buldyrev, H. E. Stanley and S. Havlin. 2012. Networks formed from interdependent networks. *Nature Physics* 8:40–48.

Hahn, M. W., and R. A. Bentley. 2003. Drift as a mechanism for cultural change: an example from baby names. *Proceedings of the Royal Society* B270:S1–S4.

Helbing, D. 2010. *Systemic Risks in Society and Economics*. Geneva: International Risk Governance Council.

Helbing, D. 2011. FuturICT—new science and technology to manage our complex, strongly connected world. Preprint (available at http://arxiv.org/abs/1108.6131).

Helbing, D., and W. Yu. 2009. The outbreak of cooperation among success-driven individuals under noisy conditions. *Proceedings of the National Academy of Sciences USA* 106:3680–3685.

Helbing, D., H. Ammoser and C. Kühnert. 2005. Disasters as extreme events and the importance of network interactions for disaster response management. In *Extreme Events in Nature and Society* (ed. S. Albeverio, V. Jentsch and H. Kantz). Springer.

Kydland, F. E., and E. C. Prescott. 1982. Time to build and aggregate fluctuations. *Econometrica* 50:1345–1370.

Laloux, L., P. Cizeau, J.-P. Bouchaud and M. Potters. 1999. Noise dressing of financial correlation matrices. *Physics Review Letters* 83:1467–1471.

Laloux, L., P. Cizeau, J.-P. Bouchaud and M. Potters. 2000. Random matrix theory and financial correlations. *International Journal of Theoretical and Applied Finance* 3:391–397.

Laury, J. S. E., G. R. Lewis and P. Ormerod. 1978. Properties of macroeconomic models of the UK economy: a comparative study. *National Institute Economic Review* 81:52–72.

Lucas, R. E. 1976. Econometric policy evaluation: a critique. *Carnegie–Rochester Conference Series on Public Policy* 1:19–46.

Maddison, A. 1995. *Monitoring the World Economy 1820–1992*. Paris: OECD.

155

Mantegna, R. N., and H. E. Stanley. 2000. *An Introduction to Econophysics: Correlations and Complexity in Finance.* Cambridge University Press.

Markowitz, H. M. 1952. Portfolio selection. *Journal of Finance* 7:77–91.

Ormerod, P. 2010a. Risk, recessions and the resilience of the capitalist economies. *Risk Management* 12:83–99.

Ormerod, P. 2010b. The current crisis and the culpability of macroeconomic theory. *Twenty-First Century Society: Journal of the Academy of Social Sciences* 5:5–18.

Ormerod, P., and R. Colbaugh. 2006. Cascades of failure and extinction in evolving complex systems. *Journal of Artificial Societies and Social Simulation* 9(4): 9.

Ormerod, P., and E. Evans. 2011. *Ex ante* prediction of cascade sizes on networks of agents facing binary outcomes. Preprint (arXiv:1103.3457).

Plerou, V., P. Gopikrishnan, B. Rosenow, L. A. N. Amaral and H. E. Stanley. 1999. Universal and non-universal properties of cross-correlations in financial time series. *Physics Review Letters* 83:1471.

Ramey, V. A. 2011. Can government purchases stimulate the economy? *Journal of Economic Literature* 49:673–685.

Reinhart, C. M., and K. S. Rogoff. 2009. *This Time Is Different: Eight Centuries of Financial Folly.* Princeton University Press.

Rendell, L., R. Boyd, D. Cownden, M. Enquist, K. Eriksson, M. W. Feldman, L. Fogarty, S. Ghirlanda, T. Lillicrap and K. N. Laland. 2010. Why copy others? Insights from the social learning strategies tournament. *Science* 328:208–213.

Schelling, T. C. 1973. Hockey helmets, concealed weapons, and daylight saving: a study of binary choices with externalities. *Journal of Conflict Resolution* 17: 381–428.

Simon, H. A. 1955. A behavioral model of rational choice. *Quarterly Journal of Economics* 69:99–118.

Tovar, C. E. 2009. DSGE models and central banks. *Economics E-Journal* 3: dx.doi.org/10.5018/economics-ejournal.ja.2009-16.

Tversky, A., and D. Kahneman. 1974. Judgment under uncertainty: heuristics and biases. *Science* 185:1124–1131.

PART 4

REFORM OF UNDERGRADUATE ECONOMICS COURSES IN THE UNITED KINGDOM

Teaching and Research in a UK University

By Michael McMahon

THE PROBLEM AS I SEE IT

The Economics Network, a body which promotes high standards and best practice in teaching economics in UK universities, conducts a biannual survey of economics students. One common complaint, among many positives, is that students are generally discontented with the amount of contact they have with academics at university. The surveys also reveal a view that some lecturers are of low quality. These problems are particularly acute at top research institutions.

Here is a selection of the quotes from the *National Economics Students Survey 2010 Report*.[1]

- 'Expected more interaction with lecturers.'
- 'Some lectures are extremely pointless to go to as reading on your own would be much easy and FUN [sic].'
- 'I feel too much teaching is left to yourself!'

The Economics Network also conducts a survey of lecturers and some quotes from the equivalent lecturers' survey follow.[2]

- 'Motivation of students is often to pass the exam rather than to learn.'
- 'Too many students who are not well prepared and don't want to work to learn.'

This chapter builds on the views I expressed in my Ted X Warwick talk on 5 March 2011. That talk can be watched online at http://tedxtalks.ted.com/video/TEDxWarwick-Dr-Michael-McMahon. All views are my own and not in any way necessarily those of any institution that I work, or have worked, for.

[1] Available at www.economicsnetwork.ac.uk/projects/stud_survey2010.pdf.

[2] Available at www.economicsnetwork.ac.uk/projects/lec_survey2009.pdf.

- 'We're caught between the devil and the deep blue sea. The university has a policy on contact hours and class sizes. Given the challenging outlook in terms of public finances, it is likely that student/staff ratios will rise further over the next five years. With pressure to conduct research that maintains our position in the top 5, something has to give.'

The first two quotes from the lecturers' survey reveal that academics are increasingly frustrated by their students' attitudes, motivation and the perceived need for spoon feeding. Of course, this description does not refer to all students but it certainly must capture more than just one or two. The final quote captures the feeling that academics, especially at top research institutions, are being pushed to do more on the teaching side while also maintaining high levels of productivity in terms of research output.

Top departments are therefore being pulled in different directions by their students and their academics. To achieve the required level of research output, academics need time; but students want that time in order to feel like they are getting the education that they deserve (and are now paying for).

A Framework in Which to Think about the Problem

Rather than just react emotively (in favour of either side) about these trade-offs and tussles, we need a framework in which to structure our thoughts. I will start by trying to analyse the incentives of lecturers to focus on research and then turn to some low-cost approaches to teaching that can help improve outcomes for everyone.

Lecturer Incentives

Suppose you present a student with a choice about how to allocate their time between two courses that will be marked in different ways, as follows.

(1) A typical university offering: lectures and seminars, two 2,000 word essays each worth 10% of the final mark, and a final exam taking up the remaining 80%.

(2) A pass–fail lecture course examined by a 2,000 word essay.

If the degree result depended on the score in the first course but was conditional on passing the second, most students would sensibly spend enough time on the second to ensure a safe pass and would then spend all their remaining time on the first course.

It turns out that the incentives for academics—who must split their time between the main tasks of teaching, administration and research—are not so different. At top research institutions, it is research that really pays off for career progression; the natural response of the academic is to just do enough to get by in the other tasks while focusing on the high-reward research.

These incentives feed into the benefits side of the lecturer decision. In terms of the other benefits to the academic, there is the chance of promotion, the satisfaction derived from professional pride of teaching well, and the opportunity to win teaching prizes. The problem is that we know that some of these benefits are very small (for example, it is basically impossible to get promoted on the basis of one's teaching), and the reality is that in the eyes of some top researchers good teaching may send a negative signal: teaching well may harm your chances of promotion if it means that you get allocated more teaching (which limits research time) or if it sends a signal that you are not a serious researcher because you obviously put too much time into your teaching.

Having thought about the benefits, what are the costs of generating better teaching outcomes? The costs are mostly time spent on lesson preparation (including the fixed costs of changing material or modules), time spent on delivery (basically, the same amount of 'face-time' is needed whether one is teaching well or poorly), and time spent on post-lecture activities, which includes dealing with questions immediately after class, office hours, feedback and recovery time.

This basic framework of costs and benefits allows us to start thinking about ways to encourage better teaching; institutions determine the benefits and some of the costs, while the lecturers and students have much greater input to the costs. Taking the role that the institution can play as a starting point and then questioning whether the academics and students can themselves play a driving role in the necessary changes, I conclude that academics and students have a key role to play. I believe we can probably achieve better outcomes without either group expending a great deal of extra effort.

THE INSTITUTIONAL SOLUTION

Acknowledging that lecturers will respond when their incentives change, one suggestion is that the institutions should simply alter the system to put much greater priority on teaching and less on research.

161

In thinking about this, it is important to ask two questions that anyone, and particularly students, might ask of departments and of the system that currently exists.

(1) Why do departments not change the incentives on offer in order to prioritize teaching and force academics to be more available to their students?

(2) Why does the research done by academics matter to students?

The answers to both questions are related. In relation to the first question, if academics have to spend more time teaching, they will spend less time on research. This lowering of research output hurts the department's reputation and, therefore, its budget. As for the second question, it seems to me like a classic problem: you want your institution to have the best reputation, to be highly ranked, to be seen to have the best people on its staff, to employ advisors to the government, and so on, but while you are there, you want the staff to put research on hold to teach you.

The problem with this plan is that most academics are in the profession to do research and there is healthy competition for good researchers. If your institution made everyone teach forty hours per week, then most of the good researchers would leave and the reputation of the institution, in terms of the quality of people there, would fall. Would students be so excited about coming to study at a place that did not have such a good reputation?

Moreover, although the increases in fees and the need to do well in the National Student Survey are putting pressure on institutions to emphasize teaching more, funding cuts are also putting extra pressure on the research side. A large amount of the new net fee revenue (fees less bursaries, scholarships, etc.) is offset by money the government previously gave to institutions but has now withdrawn.

One way in which departments can improve things is to allocate resources more efficiently to maximize teaching outcomes while allowing all those who are research active (and good) to do the research but also ensure we keep students happiest. For example, institutions should allow the best lecturers to deliver more lectures without requiring them to do the extra marking and administration that goes with teaching an extra course. The marking, for instance, could be done by those who have proven themselves to be less able (or willing) to teach well. Furthermore, departments can hire full-time administrative staff who can share the administrative burden, allowing lecturers to free up more time for research.

The Lecturer Solution

The idea that lecturers will just put more effort in without changes to either the benefits or the costs or both is unrealistic. So if the institutions will not or cannot change the benefits, perhaps lecturers would improve their teaching if the costs to them of doing so could be lowered.

One obstacle to pedagogical change is that lecturers will not want to spend the time needed on preparation and delivery. Clickers, interactive virtual learning environments[3] and classroom games are all great and students mostly love them,[4] but I fear they are only adopted by those who so enjoy teaching that the additional costs are irrelevant. Others, who perceive the costs to be high, may be pushed further away from trying to teach better.

My approach, which I call 'coaching economics', is about doing low-cost, simple things that make a big difference to outcomes. In fact, I think that a small additional up-front cost during the preparation of a session can significantly reduce the amount of time spent answering questions after lectures (by email, in office hours, and so on). All of this frees up time for more research.

These low-cost techniques are easy things like managing expectations and setting ground rules. Be clear on how you will teach and what the students can expect in terms of interaction: when and how you can be gotten hold of, etc. In class it can be as simple as setting clear objectives for each session. Tell students what is coming and how it fits into the course. Tell them what is exciting and, especially, tell them what material is boring but important. Outside of class, let them know why your office hours are at particular times and that you will not answer every email within two hours but rather will batch the answers together to limit the interruptions to your research.

Lecturers can also enthuse students by taking an interest in them and relating things to their interests. Active learning is important and is easier for the lecturer, so try to get students engaged with the material and with each other and never let them hide behind the answer 'I don't know'.

---

[3]A clicker is a hand-held device that allows students to respond to questions during a lecture. A virtual learning environment includes web-based access to course content, grades, assessments and so on. It also allows students and teacher to interact.

[4]Although, as I have shown in a research paper on the effectiveness of classroom games, not all students are equally impressed by the use of classroom games and their use can (wrongly) emphasize certain messages over other messages that are as important. I conclude that these teaching tools, like all teaching tools, need to be used with care, and they are not a guarantee of better teaching outcomes along any dimension.

Lecturers must also realize that many students see university as simply a stepping stone to some desirable career. Like a coach who helps players with their all-round fitness while teaching them a specific skill, so too lecturers must stress the numerous transferable skills, on top of any specific knowledge, that students can develop in the course of a degree in economics. Students need to realize that all of these transferable skills make them much more employable so lecturers need to tell them this (I have found that it actually helps with their motivation levels).

Finally, it must be understood that no one concentrates perfectly for a whole hour. Lecturers need to vary their delivery and interrupt the material with questions and stories; it will help those who are lost to get back on board.

I have a number of other suggestions but this is not the place to discuss my other ideas or the philosophy of 'coaching economics'.[5] The bottom line is that I believe there are a number of low-cost measures that can both improve the learning experience for students and free up time for academics to do research.

THE STUDENT SOLUTION

Of course, the final stakeholders, the students, also have an important role to play. In fact, I believe that students have the key role in determining their own university experience and especially what they learn.

Students must realize that education is not something that is done *to* you (despite the use of the expression 'I was educated at X'). In this sense, it is not like a tummy tuck for people trying to lose weight. Rather, it requires effort and immersion in the subject. Lectures are just one input and not necessarily the most important one. In other words, university education is less a quick fix like plastic surgery and more of a long haul like gym membership: you get access to the material and strategies to help you through, but you have to pick yourself up by the love handles and do the work!

Nor is it personal training, either. We do not tell students exactly when to study or exactly how to answer the questions—often I do not even circulate the 'correct answer'. In many cases there are not unique right

---

[5] The interested reader can read the many pieces that I have written on this topic on my university web page at www2.warwick.ac.uk/fac/soc/economics/staff/academic/mcmahon/research. Of particular interest will be 'Coaching economics' (2007), 'Employability, transferable skills and student motivation' (2007) and 'Reflections on my teaching' (2010).

answers, just views that the student needs to support with evidence, reasoning and logic. This independence of learning and thinking is what sets university learning apart from school.

Another way in which students can play a role is by being prepared and understanding the pressure that academics are under to do research. They must appreciate the importance of learning for themselves and engaging with their fellow students—they can learn a lot from each other.

Of course, you should make good use of your lecturers. They will be only too happy to help you when you are stuck, if it is obvious you have tried to resolve the problem on your own. If students come to see me during my office hours and say, 'I missed the lecture so what happened?', they cannot expect me to repeat the material for them.

Instead they should come and say, for example:

> I missed the lecture but I got the notes, and I spoke to a few people about the material. I understand most of it except for slide 17 where you discuss the role of banks in liquidity provision and you talk about working capital constraints. My friends and I checked these books but we are still confused about this step in the logic of the argument. Can you help explain this bit?

Students should take notes more often and refer back to them later. Lecturers already make students' lives easier by providing lots of resources online, but students need to use these resources carefully. They need to discuss material with classmates, think about it, read. And then they need to approach the lecturer with a sensible well-researched question:

> I thought you said X but I have discussed it with others and, having read the book, I now see that X doesn't make much sense if I think about it like step 1, step 2, etc. So am I missing a step in the logic, or does it not mean X?

This is easy to answer and discuss; an academic may actually enjoy this sort of interaction.

Finally, as alluded to above when discussing transferable skills and employability, students need to understand that a university education is much more than just a transfer of specific academic knowledge, or even ways of thinking. University provides a wonderful environment in which students can practise thinking and writing, take risks and explore new ideas, learn to answer questions having not been told the answer nor had time to think, learn to work with people from diverse backgrounds and with different outlooks on topics. All of these opportunities provide golden material to use in job interviews and in job applications.

CHAPTER NINETEEN

An Aside on What Makes a 'Great Teacher'

Before I conclude, let me just give a few thoughts on what makes a great teacher. Just like great sports coaches, a great teacher does not have to do popular things. By giving out the exam in advance and giving everyone great grades, I would have a popular and easy course but no one would learn anything apart from, 'Take Michael's course, it's dead easy to get good marks in!'

Instead, a great teacher should

- motivate students and impart their own passion for the subject and
- engage students and get them interested in the material.

They must make difficult material easy to follow. In delivering their course, they will give students a great foundation by not just providing the material but also by allowing students to develop independence of thought, as well as other skills including confidence, the ability to think on their feet and more.

Of course, simply looking at scores on student surveys will not capture whether teaching achieves this aim. Students often do not, at this stage, recognize deferred realization of benefits. Some of my approaches are not popular with students, but I like them. I like the challenges that students face and they should experience these in a risk-free environment. I tell them this and they, sometimes begrudgingly, understand—and in the long run they will see the benefits.

Conclusion

The problem I identified is that the incentives as they currently are push academics to do research, and the perceived lack of teaching effort seems to frustrate students, who feel that they are owed more time with the academics. My solutions involve departments properly optimizing their resources for the best outcomes; academics engaging more with students through low-cost but highly effective teaching, which adds a lot of value to student learning; and students helping themselves and the academics in their departments by embracing independent and collegial learning.

166

Disseminating the Changes Already Underway in Higher Education Economics

By John Sloman

Many changes to economics education are already underway. If these changes are widely disseminated, so that universities can learn from each other's successes and difficulties in responding to concerns about the relevance of the economics education they provide, there could be a substantial gain in the quality and employability of economics graduates.

This essay focuses on two issues: what should be taught and how should it be taught. It concentrates especially on the latter, which has received much less attention despite being, as I will argue, of crucial importance if economics graduates are to be equipped with the knowledge and skills needed to make them effective analysts, problem solvers and advisers in their work.

THE CURRICULUM

There seems to be a wide degree of agreement that many courses lack a historical perspective, and that students do not gain sufficient insight into the historical context in which theories and policies have developed.

Paradigms are adopted that reflect current or recent contexts, such as the 'Great Moderation' from the early 1990s to the mid 2000s. The assumptions may be valid in particular contexts, but they often cease to be valid in new political or institutional circumstances, like financial markets characterized by the rapid development and spread of collateralized debt obligations. Models that reflected the circumstances of the recent past (such as the dynamic stochastic general equilibrium model, or the conflation of the IS and modified Phillips curve models with a monetary policy rule based on inflation targeting or the pursuit of a Taylor rule) may therefore cease to be relevant as circumstances change, especially when the changes are extreme. Existing macro models have typically assumed well-functioning markets and too little attention has been paid

167

to leverage, systemic risk, global imbalances, the lack of macroprudential policies and the instability of the system as a whole.

A greater knowledge of the development of the models being taught in their historical context—a blend of economic history and the history of economic thought—incorporated into existing modules, rather than as a freestanding module, would help to inoculate against the complacency of believing that consensus models are universal, or even remain relevant within the current context, when the seeds of future problems may be being sown. Boom and bust might have been temporarily defeated in the battle of the 1990s and early 2000s. The war, however, was not won.

The development of the discipline of economics involves a dialectical process. The thesis represented by standard textbook models (themselves a synthesis of earlier conflicts between schools of thought) does not adapt quickly enough to take account of the antithetical developments in financial instruments, regulatory structures, institutional developments, global imbalances, and so on. A crisis is ultimately experienced. Examples from the past were the failure of the classical economists to explain the Great Depression, the failure of Keynesian economics and the Phillips curve analysis to explain the stagflation of the 1970s, and the failure of the dynamic stochastic general equilibrium model to explain the crisis of 2007/8. What then emerges from the crisis is a synthesis. Models are adapted or new models developed; assumptions are modified. The new synthesis may then become the new standard model until the cycle is repeated.

In microeconomics, the process is generally less dramatic, as the failure of models to explain behaviour or economic performance does not result in large-scale political crisis and the fall of governments. Of course, there are political implications, even though these are not ones of crisis management. Microeconomists advising politicians must have incentives and their impact on human behaviour at the heart of policy proposals. So, as with macroeconomics, the process is similarly dialectical. The mounting evidence from psychologists, the marketing industry and experimental economists that human rationality may be bounded in ways that are subject to manipulation—and that asymmetry of information may severely curtail efficient decision making—has led to explanations that are antithetical to standard neoclassical microeconomics. The failure of the standard general equilibrium models, based on the assumption of maximizing behaviour, is apparent in many contexts. The models are thus amended— or, more radically, discarded—by behavioural economists. The revolution may be slower, but paradigms do change.

So are these changes reflected in the curriculum? There are two elements to the answer: what is taught within modules and what is written in textbooks.

Changes to Curricula

If you look at the course outlines for an economics undergraduate or taught postgraduate degree today, they will seem very different from those of 20 years ago. Most universities have to undergo periodic programme review, which entails degrees and their modules being subject to a peer review process, including the involvement of external assessors or advisers. There is pressure on lecturers to ensure that their modules and reading lists are up to date.

Sometimes the changes are relatively minor, but at times of rapid economic change and adjustments in theories to reflect these changes, many lecturers will incorporate these changes into their modules. Of course, there is often a time lag before these changes are embedded, but most lecturers will at least want to refer to current economic circumstances and to the ability, or lack of ability, of standard models to explain these circumstances.

Some lecturers will be more radical in their adaptation of the syllabus, meaning that there will be a range of approaches adopted. It is important for information on such changes to be disseminated around the economics academic community. Unfortunately, whilst previously such changes were open to inspection from outside a university, most module details are now hidden in a virtual learning environment, such as Blackboard or Moodle. Dissemination is not easy.

One answer to this problem is to set up communities at the subdiscipline level to share teaching materials, such as module outlines, reading lists, seminar activities and past assessments. The idea is not to copy each other's materials, but to share ideas about syllabus design and content, and about teaching, learning and assessment practices. The Economics Network has set up fourteen such communities under its Teaching Resources for Undergraduate Economics (TRUE) project.[1] Additional subject communities could be set up and are likely to be more successful if led by an enthusiastic and innovative lecturer who is respected in that particular field.

---

[1] The health economics education community at www.economicsnetwork.ac.uk/health is a good example.

The Economics Network conducts biennial surveys of economics lecturers, biennial surveys of economics students and periodic surveys of economics alumni and of employers of economists. More than two-thirds of students in recent years found the content of their degree to be 'relevant' or 'largely relevant' to the real world: the percentages for the last four surveys are 66.8% (2006), 69.3% (2008), 71.7% (2010) and 69.5% (2012).[2] Nevertheless, there was a substantial minority who were dissatisfied with the relevance of the contents of their degree:

> The focus was mostly from an academic, research-based standpoint. During the entire four-year economics course, we didn't really focus on the financial crisis, which would seem to be one of the most important economic events in history! Much emphasis was placed on old, outdated theories that defy common sense.

> I thought there would be more emphasis on the current economic climate.... My course tends to get bogged down in the maths and formulas. I was expecting a more practical approach to economics, with the emphasis on developing economic thinking and intuition.

> There should be much more emphasis placed on real-world examples. I would have liked to have learned more about the financial crisis through an economic lens. They should really think why people are taking the subject. I for one am not taking econ [sic] to be an academic. I would like to have a fairly comprehensive idea of how an economy works and is influenced by political and other factors. That would have benefited my life. Learning about game theory (Cournot duopoly) is one area which did not benefit my life. Why would I really care about a complex (probably non-existent) occurrence?

> It certainly turned me off doing a masters. I was all set to do a one-year course for an MA, but not any more! I would much rather be out in the world really applying economics and making some money.

The surveys have shown that undergraduates' satisfaction with the relevance of their degree decreases as they progress through their studies. In the 2012 survey, the percentages finding their course relevant or largely relevant were 78.0% in year one, 70.9% in year two, 60.0% in year three and 54.1% in year four (in Scotland). The figure was 69.5% for postgraduates, which is the same as the undergraduate average.

---

[2] These figures come from the answers to question 22 of the *National Economics Students Survey 2012 Report*: 'How relevant to the real world do you find the content of the degree?' (www.economicsnetwork.ac.uk/projects/surveys#National_Surveys_of_Economics_Students).

The question for the discipline is how to disseminate good practice and to motivate lecturers to make changes to their syllabuses that reflect recent developments.

Changes to Textbooks

There is inevitably a lag before textbooks reflect current theoretical developments. Partly this is the production cycle and partly it is the need for the 'dust to have settled' somewhat before theories can be presented in a form accessible to students and embedded in a structured presentation of the subject. But these lags are not that long. Most textbooks are revised on a three- or four-year cycle and competitive pressures on textbook authors encourage them to reflect the latest economic developments and the theoretical and policy responses.

Core textbooks in micro and macro at all levels do change. The texts of today do reflect the theoretical developments that have taken place over the years—perhaps too slowly when change is very rapid—but at least they reflect the institutional and policy changes relatively quickly, even if the presentation of developed theories takes longer. But even new theoretical developments are reflected relatively rapidly, normally juxtaposed with more standard theories and with their explanatory and predictive power compared.

The Ever-More-Crowded Curriculum

A problem for both lecturers and textbook authors is that there is always pressure to include new theoretical, institutional and policy developments but at the same time there is natural pressure to retain, or simply adapt, existing material.

Textbook reviewers typically want the author to add this, that and the other, take nothing out, and reduce the length of the book to keep the price down and prevent students from complaining about its size. Although such conjuring tricks can be pulled off by careful pruning, there is always the danger that students will be expected to know more and more.

It is the same for lecturers. There is pressure to add material to reflect the developments of the subject, as well as to retain what was there before in order to contextualize recent developments. The danger is that students will be expected to know more material; but knowing more may mean understanding less.

Lecturers feel the need to cover the full syllabus—a syllabus that tends to grow. But covering material in lectures or on reading lists does not mean that students have learned it, still less that they are able to apply it in unfamiliar, real-world contexts. And if lecturers are to be encouraged to include more economic history and history of economic thought in their curricula, then what is to give? Preferably the answer is the amount of material rather than the depth of understanding.

Part of the challenge for lecturers, therefore, is to reduce the volume of material while making their courses relevant and challenging to students. This is a judgement that individual lecturers have to make, but they are helped by being able to share solutions with colleagues within their universities and with those teaching the same subject(s) elsewhere through subdiscipline communities—whether online or at research conferences, where one or more teaching sessions could be introduced.

But producing economics graduates fit for the labour market is not just a question of ensuring that the curricula are up to date. It is also a question of ensuring that teaching and learning help develop the knowledge and skills that both lecturers and employers, and students themselves, would like graduates to possess. This includes not only the knowledge of current theories and their development but also knowledge of the global institutional and political environment. Students need research and inductive skills, problem-solving skills and the ability to relate economic theories and concepts to messy real-world situations for which data are limited and where agency problems and problems of information asymmetry abound.

The development of such knowledge and skills depends crucially on teaching method, to which I turn now.

Teaching Method

Students can be motivated by charismatic teaching, but not all teachers are blessed with charismatic personalities. Nevertheless, there is a range of teaching techniques and class types that can motivate students and help them develop the knowledge and skills that will make them valuable employees—or employers.

Central to good teaching is encouraging students to think, reflect and question. Spoon feeding that encourages regurgitation is generally regarded as being of limited value to students. Unfortunately, there are incentives that encourage lecturers to do just that. A crowded curriculum tends to encourage racing through material, with the students cramming for exams. Pressure on lecturers to get good pass rates—a pressure that is increased by various quality assurance procedures—encourages making assessments predictable and 'teaching to the exam'. Even when the exam involves calculation, rather than the mere rehearsing of arguments or theories, repeated drilling sessions where students are given highly stylized problems in class only to be given exactly the same ones, but with different numbers, in exams is a form of spoon feeding.

The problem can be made worse when student choices are increased. Lecturers teaching optional modules want students to choose the modules they teach. If one of their modules does not run, they are likely to have to spend time preparing an alternative module. If a module is seen as relatively easy to pass and relatively predictable, students are likely to be encouraged to choose it. *Ex post*, students might regret not having been sufficiently challenged, but *ex ante*, the likelihood of doing well in the module is a major driver of student choice.

One solution is to adopt procedures where lecturers discuss their module curricula and teaching and assessment methods with their colleagues. Another would be to require lecturers to specify learning objectives in student-friendly language and to discuss such objectives and the means of achieving them with their students. Most universities do require lecturers to identify learning aims and objectives in their module documentation, but this is normally in educational terminology, which has little buy-in from cynical staff, who quickly learn how to play the game of saying what will satisfy quality assurance procedures.

At the core of an approach to encourage more effective and deeper learning—where students are encouraged to think, reflect and question— is the need to make the learning process active rather than passive and to encourage students to take more responsibility for their learning. But increasing demands on lecturers tend to militate against this.

Demands on Lecturers

The traditional mix of lectures and seminars/tutorials has tended to evolve to reflect the problems of having larger cohorts of students to teach and the pressures of research. A central problem facing departments is how to be more cost-effective.

As far as the cost element is concerned, the solution for many departments has been larger class sizes and an increase in the ratio of lectures to seminars. In this way, class contact hours for lecturers can be kept down (class contact hours being the standard unit of account for allocating staffing). But if lectures are conducted in the traditional form of one-way communication, with no student interaction, then passive learning is likely to increase.

If seminars are used in the traditional way of either going through pre-prepared problem sets or an individual student presenting a paper, an increase in class size increases the scope for free-riding and students get less individual attention from the tutor. What is more, the traditional seminar forms may also encourage passive learning. If a seminar is used to go through a problem set, then students are there largely to check on the accuracy of the work they have done outside the class rather than to problem solve actively within the class. If students have not done the work, then their role may be reduced to that of a passive onlooker. The problem can be even worse with a traditional paper presentation, where the seminar often deteriorates into a discussion between the paper presenter and the tutor. Again, the other students may simply be passive onlookers, unwilling to contribute comments, especially if they have not done the reading, preferring to devote their efforts to the seminar in which they themselves have to present.

Another solution to larger student numbers has been the increasing use of postgraduate students as teaching assistants. While graduate teaching assistants (GTAs) are not necessarily poorer teachers than established lecturers, their lack of experience (combined, frequently, with language and cultural problems) provides challenges for a department—challenges that are often inadequately dealt with by training, monitoring and support by experienced staff or by peer support by fellow GTAs. If curricula are to reflect recent theoretical developments and are to be more closely related to real-world issues, then this might put further strains on the GTA system of seminar teaching.

But cost-effectiveness is not just about reducing costs. It is important to focus on how larger classes can be made more effective and on how staff time can be allocated differently to improve student learning.

A Focus on Student Learning

An important element in effective student learning is for lecturers to identify what they want students to gain from the module and then to articulate that to students—not in terms of a sterile list of 'learning outcomes', expressed in formal educational language, but rather in terms of how students should be able to apply the knowledge they gain from the module in a variety of academic, employment and other contexts. The learning objectives should be part of an informal contract between lecturer and students that can be revisited as the module progresses.

174

There are various ways of doing this.

- Draw up an informal work contract in the first seminar, where students identify what they expect (a) from the tutor, (b) from fellow students in the class and (c) of themselves as members of a learning community.
- Encourage the development of a learning community outside class. The use of discussion boards, wikis or Facebook groups helps to build such communities and allows online communication between members.
- Get and give frequent feedback on the progress of students' learning. This can be done in class through informal questionnaires, through the use of audience response systems, i.e. 'clickers' (see below), through quick tests or quizzes and through students engaging in personal development planning or group planning and reflection.

It is also important to focus the activities in class on the process of student learning in order to make the process active and reflective, rather than the passive one of merely absorbing information.

Lectures

A lecturer who talks for fifty minutes (the typical length of a lecture) is not thereby ensuring that each student has learned fifty minutes' worth of material. Just because something has been covered in the lecture does not mean that students have copied it all down, let alone understood it all. Listening passively to a lecturer, however engaging that lecturer might be, is subject to diminishing returns to time. A salutary lesson for lecturers (and a very useful exercise for students) is to take a break for five minutes during the lecture and have students compare the notes they have taken with those of their neighbour. Students can gain considerably from this process, identifying gaps and misunderstandings, whether they are doing the assessing of being assessed. If the lecturer has sight of these notes, perhaps by moving around the room as the students are doing the exercise, immediate feedback is available. It will be obvious that not everything has been taken down or understood.

Lectures can be made a much more active learning experience if the lecturer trades some talking time for student activity: perhaps ten to fifteen minutes of activity in a fifty-minute lecture. Students can be set small problems or multiple-choice questions. These can be answered using clickers, with the results of the votes being displayed in PowerPoint by the lecturer at the front. Such interaction is fun, motivating and helps embed learning. It also gives immediate feedback to the lecturer on the extent of student understanding.

In lectures where models or theories are developed, the students can be asked, 'what would happen if...?', or they could write down the next line of a proof. In lectures discussing policy, the students could be asked to identify advantages and disadvantages of particular measures before the lecturer goes through them.

Showing a brief video, for example from the BBC News website, can illustrate an economic issue and give students a break from listening to the lecturer. One or two brief questions on the video could be posed at the end of it.

Lectures can easily be recorded using screen capture software such as Camtasia, with the audio track being linked to what students see on screen: a PowerPoint display or a website, for example. Students can play this back later, and be set work reflecting on the material.

Formal note takers can be assigned to lectures on a rotating basis, with the note taker posting the notes on a discussion board. Threaded discussions can then be contributed to by the whole student cohort, or group by group, possibly with the lecturer responding. The time taken for the lecturer to do this may be less than the time spent answering individual queries by students without such a discussion board.

Seminars

If attending seminars is to involve active learning, it is important that students do work in the seminar and not simply report on work done outside it. Take the case of a problem set. If students have prepared answers to a problem set as homework, then they could be given additional questions to work through during the seminar, either individually or in pairs or threes. These could be the same as the homework questions but with different numbers. By working in pairs or in threes, the students who have got the correct answers to the homework can teach the students who have struggled: there is a two-way gain from this process.

The above is just one model. The principle is a simple one: lecturers should try to avoid their seminars becoming simply sterile reporting sessions, with little in the way of active and reflective learning.

In the case of what would have been a paper presentation session, a more active experience for the class would be to transform this into a debate. Students could take pre-prepared positions, which might be those of journal articles arguing opposing theories, or different positions in the case of policy debates. An element of theatre helps to motivate and engage students. Formats could include a formal debate, a trial, a panel quizzing witnesses (as in the BBC's *Moral Maze* on Radio 4), or role playing.

There is also considerable scope for classroom experiments, especially in microeconomics. Such experiments are increasingly being used to great effect by many economics departments, and they give students insight into many situations involving economic interaction and motivation and can illustrate a number of gaming and market outcomes. Various macroeconomic simulations are also available, but there are fewer of them.[3]

Adapting Class Sizes and Structures to Learning Objectives

If questions in class have a correct answer rather than requiring students to give a reasoned opinion, large classes may be an efficient means of achieving the learning objectives. For example, large-scale workshops can be used for more technical questions and for manipulating models. Students can be given a worksheet as they enter the room and they can then work on questions in twos and threes. After completing, say, fifteen minutes' worth of questions, the lecturer could go through the answers from the front, perhaps getting students to use clickers first so that their answers can be displayed. While students are working, one or two GTAs, plus the lecturer, could move around the room tackling student queries. This is an effective use of GTAs, who are likely to be better at teaching individuals than they would be at teaching a whole class. If the workshop takes place in a tiered lecture theatre, having a rule that every third row of seats is left vacant allows the GTAs to visit every student in the room. I ran such workshops with a colleague for many years and they were very well received. Students thoroughly enjoyed them and attendance was very high.

If the original allocation for a module were one or two lectures and one seminar per week per student, then adding a workshop for the whole cohort would add only two to three hours of staff time. If seminars were then held fortnightly and focused on policy issues, where structured student debate was important, there would be a net saving in staff time in core modules with large numbers of students, and yet also an increase of half an hour of class time for students. What is more, class size and structure would be appropriately aligned to learning outcomes.

---

[3] See 'Classroom Experiments & Games' on the Economics Network website at www .economicsnetwork.ac.uk/themes/games.

Additional timetabled student classes could be held online, with either no member of staff present or a member of staff moving between a number of online groups held simultaneously. Such online classes could be formally structured, using a discussion board with clear rules of engagement. Perhaps the first one or two could be held in a computer lab in order to answer any queries and establish the 'rules of the game'. Questions could be posted by the tutor to the discussion board in advance, perhaps with links to current articles or data, and students could make initial posts to the board prior to the class. The timetabled class could then involve students responding to each other's posts. Again, this is a way of increasing student contact without increasing the amount of time staff spend with students (see, for example, Sloman 2002).

Peer-to-Peer Learning

Many forms of peer-to-peer learning by students involve little effort by lecturers, bar some relatively small set-up and administrative costs. The important thing is to explain to students how they can learn from each other and the benefits to be gained. The process could be formal, with students learning in pre-allocated groups, with allocated tasks. Group coordinators could be chosen by the students and these coordinators would ensure that the groups met, either physically or online.

Group work could form part of assessment, as long as free-rider issues were addressed. The Economics Network has a number of case studies considering the most effective ways of using group work and assessing groups (see, for example, Watkins 2005).

Problem-Based Learning

Problem-based learning (PBL) is widely used in many disciplines, including medicine, engineering and management. It was pioneered at McMaster University in Canada and at Maastricht University in the Netherlands, where all courses (including economics) use PBL.[4] The principle is that students should be problem solvers and should initially be presented with problems to research and analyse. Theory is learned or taught in the context of problem solving, which immediately contextualizes theory and helps students to understand the role of theory in explanation, analysis

---

[4]See, for example, www.maastrichtuniversity.nl/web/Main/Education/EducationalMe thod/ProblemBasedLearning.htm.

and prediction. The success of PBL in motivating students and encouraging deep learning has led many disciplines to embrace it as the main learning mode, or at least as an important element in the learning process.

In PBL the role of the lecturer is that of an expert whom students can consult for information and guidance. Students work in groups and take on the roles of researchers and advisers. These roles are similar to those that many will play in employment when they graduate, and PBL therefore provides useful training for future careers. Students take responsibility for their learning.

Adopting PBL need not be costly for departments. It is not a question of all or nothing. Elements of PBL can be introduced into existing courses and there are many successful examples of this in the United Kingdom across the range of core and optional subjects, including macroeconomics, industrial economics, econometrics, development economics and economic principles. Some of these example involve an initial set of lectures, with the rest of the module being in a PBL format. There are many case studies on the Economics Network site. (See also Forsythe (2010).)

The PBL approach can be adapted to suit particular modules. For example, Steve Cook is using a project-based approach to teach econometrics at Swansea University (Cook 2011).

> The objective of the project was to develop a module which adopted a different approach to the delivery and assessment of econometrics for final year undergraduates. The underlying motivation was to produce a module driven by the twin motivations of 'learning by doing' and 'assessment by doing'. As a result, a 30 credit applied econometrics module emerged which had frequent workshops and assessment via the submission of six mini-projects—without a formal examination.
>
> Cook (2011)

Judging by student marks, student evaluations and staff enjoyment, the module has been extremely successful.

Assessment

In designing an assessment regime there is a clear tension between the views of students—who, in many universities, feel that they are underassessed and/or inappropriately assessed—and those of staff—who find marking and (especially in the more quantitative subjects) setting assessments a great burden, let alone the time taken giving feedback on assessments. The 2012 Economics Network Student Survey found that the majority of respondents felt that they would benefit from more assessment during a module, with less weight being given to the final exam. But lecturers frequently look for ways of cutting down on marking, such as through the use of multiple-choice tests or group work, with a single mark allocated to the group with perhaps some reallocation within limits by members of the group.

But there are ways of curtailing staff costs while improving student learning, as follows.

- Group work with ways of capturing the contribution of individuals: by their taking responsibility for particular parts of the report, for example, or by submitting a brief work journal.
- The introduction of peer-to-peer marking for formative assessment.
- The use of comment banks, with margin notes by the lecturer referring to specific generic comments from the bank.
- Feedback on the entire cohort, with minimal comments on individual work.
- Students being required to make their own comments on their work before submission, with the lecturer confirming or disagreeing with these comments.
- The use of mark sheets by lecturers, with scores according to how well students have met specific criteria, plus a general comment box at the end.

Then there is the question of the deployment of staff. It might be a good use of GTA time to make them marking assistants rather than teaching assistants. Their comparative advantage may lie in marking and providing feedback, providing they are given support in the process—but this support may be less time consuming than that required for teaching.

As far as feedback is concerned, this is one of the areas of most concern to students, and the element that is consistently scored lowest in the National Student Survey. But for feedback to be effective, students must engage with that which they are given. One means of encouraging this is to require them to comment on the feedback on their last piece of marked work at the start of the next and to say how they are addressing the comments in the current piece. Another way is to require students to engage in peer feedback. This could be a formal process of commenting on one or more students' work in class or it could be groups marking work submitted by previous students, such as examples of last year's exam answers (anonymized, of course).

CONCLUDING COMMENTS

There are already many examples of changes to the curriculum to reflect the economic crisis and various theoretical, institutional and structural developments, but the question is how others can be given access to these changes. Similarly, many innovations have been introduced to the teaching of economics and they have been embedded in courses or are being tried out, but what they are and what their costs and benefits are is not widely known.

The Economics Network and the journals *International Review of Economics Education* and *Journal of Economic Education* provide a great deal of information about both curriculum developments and innovative teaching, learning and assessment methods, but dissemination needs to be systematic and there needs to be buy-in by the academic economics community.

Setting up communities that develop and share open educational resources in subdisciplines is part of the solution. Another part is an increased role for representative bodies—such as the Royal Economic Society, the Conference of Heads of University Departments of Economics and various subdiscipline societies and groups—in engaging with changes to the economics curriculum and teaching methods. And a third part of the solution is for employers' bodies, such as the Government Economic Service and the Confederation of British Industry, to play a major role in the debate about the appropriateness of economics education in preparing economics students for employment.

REFERENCES

Cook, S. 2011. Project-based learning of modern econometrics. Economics Network. Available at www.economicsnetwork.ac.uk/projects/mini/cook_econo metrics.

Forsythe, F. 2010. Problem-based learning. In *The Handbook for Economics Lecturers*. Economics Network. Available at www.economicsnetwork.ac.uk/handbook/pbl.

Sloman, J. 2002. Use of virtual seminars in economic principles. Economics Network. Available at www.economicsnetwork.ac.uk/showcase/sloman_virtual).

Watkins, R. 2005. Groupwork and assessment. In *The Handbook for Economics Lecturers*. Economics Network. Available at www.economicsnetwork.ac.uk/handbook/groupwork.

CHAPTER TWENTY-ONE

Good Economists Need More than Economics: The Multidisciplinary LSE100 Course

By Jonathan Leape

Many reflections on economics following the financial crisis of 2008 have highlighted concerns about how economics is taught. One concern is that the education of economists has been too narrow and too insular, often leaving our students ill prepared to confront complex 'real-world' problems. This is reinforced by a second concern: that economics students receive too little grounding in reasoning and problem solving based on observations and evidence, or in other words *inductive* approaches. We tend to teach economics on the basis of strong theoretical foundations and logical reasoning from a specific set of assumptions. The seductive elegance and simplicity of this *deductive* reasoning is compounded by our tendency to dismiss inductive approaches as ad hoc. This has contributed to an education that gives short shrift to the inductive aspects of learning from assiduous observation and careful use of data and that fails to instil in our students a critical, questioning approach to the assumptions we make.[1] This lack of attention to reasoning from evidence, and from evidence-based assumptions, has been accompanied by a superficial approach to questions of causality.

I am profoundly grateful to my LSE100 colleagues, too many to mention individually, for many thought-provoking discussions over the past three years that have deepened my understanding of these issues. For insightful comments on a previous draft of this paper, I would like to thank Juljan Krause. Finally, I would like especially to thank Diane Coyle for her instrumental role in organizing the original workshop and the initiatives that have followed.

[1] Friedman (1953) famously asserted that 'theoretical models should be tested primarily by the accuracy of their predictions rather than by the reality of their assumptions'. Friedman's view has been widely challenged, however, notably by Hicks. The latter argued that economic theories change over time, reflecting the changing cultural, technological and institutional context for economic behaviour, and that economic predictions are, at best, weak claims about what will happen if all other things remain the same. What is more, as Helm (1984) puts it, 'since *ceteris* is almost never *paribus*, a particular set of observations can never, themselves, form the basis for testing an hypothesis'.

These concerns link to longstanding debates in economics. Keynes gave us the following daunting definition:

> The master-economist must possess a rare combination of gifts.... He must be mathematician, historian, statesman, philosopher—in some degree. He must understand symbols and speak in words.

Yet the trend in economics degree programmes has been to increase core requirements at the expense of such breadth. Even for those students whose ambitions fall well short of becoming a 'master-economist'—who simply wish to apply economic tools to real problems—the need for greater breadth in their economics education has become clear. With respect to the second concern, many would share Keynes's definition of economics as a 'science of thinking in terms of models joined to the art of choosing models that are relevant to the contemporary world'. But, while most undergraduate economics programmes can rightly pride themselves on their success in teaching model-based thinking, the equally important challenge of choosing the appropriate theoretical model and the associated need to learn 'bottom up' from empirical evidence, not least in assessing the assumptions made, is too often overlooked (see, for example, John Kay's chapter in this book and Eichengreen (2009)).

These concerns highlight the need to expose economics students to other disciplinary perspectives—other formal ways of thinking—as part of their degree. Not only can this provide them with something closer to the 'combination of gifts' required to engage meaningfully with real-world problems, but it can contribute to their understanding of the uses and limitations of theoretical models, as discussed below. It can also, in turn, help teach them about inductive approaches through exposure to disciplines such as history or anthropology, where such approaches are central, giving economics students a wider portfolio of perspectives to bring to bear on new problems.

One way of introducing a multidisciplinary element is through joint degrees. Joint degrees are well suited to those students whose interest in economics is matched by strong interest in another discipline and can provide them with an opportunity to develop a deep understanding of two (or more) distinct approaches. That joint degrees in politics and economics, and in philosophy, politics and economics, are thriving is testimony to the demand for such multidisciplinarity.

Another strategy is to require all economics students to take some courses in other disciplines (so-called distribution requirements). This approach also has merit. Distribution requirements can introduce students to alternative disciplinary approaches; indeed, this rationale underlies the 'liberal arts' degrees common in the United States. But they do so less systematically and deeply than joint degrees. On the other hand, joint degrees inevitably require some sacrifice in the number of economics courses taken, which is much less of an issue with the more limited distribution requirements.

However, both options suffer from the shortcoming that the different disciplines are typically studied in parallel, often as completely separate silos. As a consequence, while the student benefits from exposure to alternative disciplines, the gains in terms of her understanding of methodological issues and her critical understanding of economics may be limited.

An alternative approach has recently been adopted by the London School of Economics, which has introduced a new, multidisciplinary course that is a compulsory element in all undergraduate degrees. The course is the result of a review of the undergraduate degree programmes that revealed certain concerns shared across the social sciences. First among these was concern at a growing mismatch between the increasing specialization of many of the degree programmes and the intellectual breadth we felt an undergraduate education should provide, not least to enable our graduates to apply their disciplinary training to real-world problems. This message was reinforced by feedback from employers. Our graduates, they reported, had strong disciplinary skills—for economists, strong technical and problem-solving skills—and yet they often struggled when confronted with a new type of problem that called for different methods or a mix of approaches. Moreover, their technical competence was not consistently matched by a similar level of effectiveness in articulating arguments.

We concluded that we could address these problems, while preserving the strengths of our degree programmes, by introducing a compulsory fifth course (spread over the first and second years) that all undergraduates would take in addition to their degree requirements. The central objective of the course would be to broaden students' intellectual experience at the LSE. Some people were worried that such a course, and the additional workload involved, might risk undermining the depth of understanding achieved by the degree programmes. We believed the reverse to be true, though. We believed that, in the process of giving students greater intellectual breadth, the new course would deepen their critical understanding of their own discipline, as discussed below.

We also believed that introducing students to a variety of disciplinary approaches—to diverse 'ways of thinking'—would have a range of other benefits for their intellectual development.

A second objective of the course was to address the somewhat haphazard development of research skills across the undergraduate programmes. As we considered the skills required for the social science degrees we offer, it became clear that there was a gap between the skills we expected students to have and the support that was in place to help them develop those skills. We also concluded that there was very substantial overlap between these research-orientated skills and the transferable skills that would best serve our students after they graduate.

When the focus shifted from initial proposal to design and implementation, it was immediately evident that the new course would require a clear framework of aims and learning outcomes (see the box on the facing page). To give meaning and structure to the first aim of intellectual breadth and to integrate both the aims into an overarching set of learning outcomes, it was, in my view, useful to translate the first aim into a set of four 'methodological' skills. Using the themes of evidence, explanation and theory, the vague notion of intellectual breadth was translated into a series of skills that serve as accessible learning outcomes for students.

The first of the skills listed in the box focuses on evidence and the need for students to be able to evaluate and interpret different types of evidence, from statistical data to documentary sources, from ethnographic monographs to blogs. A strong focus on evidence underpins the emphasis given to inductive approaches on the course. The second focuses on the research process: that is, on the central role of questions in driving an iterative process between evidence, explanation and theory. Setting out the research process in this way serves to demystify research and underscore the parallels with effective learning and argumentation—which helps to promote identification, interest and commitment on the part of students. The third skill focuses on the need to think formally about the role of causal claims in social science explanations, and the fourth underscores the benefit of applying different disciplinary perspectives to a particular problem.

To this group of methodological skills were added 'information skills' and 'communication skills', both of which are central to research and study in the social sciences, while also, like the methodological skills, being important transferable skills in future employment. The inclusion of information skills stems from the recognition that, as 'digital natives', current students require a particular set of search, evaluation

The LSE100 Course: Understanding the Causes of Things

Aims

(i) To deepen and broaden students' understanding of social scientific thinking, focusing particularly on the core themes of evidence, explanation and theory.
(ii) To strengthen the critical skills that underpin the study and application of the social sciences.

Critical skills and learning outcomes

Methodological skills

(1) Evaluate and interpret evidence of different types, including documentary and other qualitative sources as well as statistical data.
(2) Explain the respective roles of, and interaction between, questions, theories, evidence and explanations in the social sciences.
(3) Identify and critically assess causal claims in social science explanations.
(4) Analyse contemporary social problems using theoretical perspectives from more than one social science discipline.

Information skills

(5) Find and access information relevant to social science problems, making use of good searching principles and techniques.
(6) Evaluate information sources, distinguishing scholarly sources from other content and critically assessing information from internet and other sources.
(7) Manage information—and reduce information overload—using online and other resources as well as appropriate citing and referencing techniques.

Communication skills

(8) Construct coherent and persuasive arguments—both orally and in writing—on current issues in the social sciences, structuring the arguments logically and supporting them with relevant evidence.
(9) Plan and deliver engaging and well-argued presentations that coherently address both question and audience.

and management skills that were not consistently being developed or supported in the way their existing degree programmes had developed. Under the heading of communication skills, primary emphasis is given to argumentation, using the rhetoric of thesis–justification–support, which supports both the methodological skills and effective communication.

The course is designed around six three-week modules, each of which focuses on an important issue of public debate, with lecturers drawn from at least two different disciplines. In the current programme, for example, these modules are the following.

- How should we manage climate change? (Economics, Political Science)
- Does culture matter? (Anthropology, Economic History)
- Why are great events so difficult to predict? (International Relations, History)
- Who caused the global financial crisis? (Economics, History, International Relations)
- Is population growth a threat or an opportunity? (Development, Social Policy)
- Who should own ideas? (Media, Law)

The use of 'big' questions serves both to motivate the exploration of different disciplinary approaches and to underscore the importance of inductive approaches in the course as a whole. In both respects, it is an approach quite different to that of joint degrees or to the use of distribution requirements to achieve intellectual breadth. In both of those cases, additional disciplinary perspectives are introduced but not confronted, so the opportunity to use direct contrasts and similarities between different disciplinary approaches to deepen students' understanding of methodological issues—and to develop a more critical understanding of their own discipline—may be lost.

While the lectures in the LSE100 course provide the intellectual structure, it is in the small weekly classes that students engage directly with the material and develop their skills and understanding. To support a high level of interaction and feedback, which is crucial to self-reflection and skill development, classes are limited to twelve students. Larger classes could certainly work, although there would, inevitably, be some reduction in the level of feedback provided and it would be somewhat more demanding in terms of the experience and skills required of the teachers. The primary emphasis in the classes is on research methods, and the classes use a highly structured, task-based approach that integrates the three key skill areas. This structure has been crucial both to making the classes effective for the wide variety of students on the course, coming from thirty-seven different degree programmes (as well as from many different backgrounds), and to enabling the class teachers to teach outside their discipline (many for the first time in their professional lives).

In the current introductory class, for example, students examine how different questions about poverty lead to different measures (e.g. the dollar-a-day measure versus the human poverty index), in turn reflecting different conceptions of poverty (based on income versus multidimensional human development), requiring different kinds of evidence, pointing to different explanations and having different policy implications. Students are then asked to critically assess the United Nations decision to adopt the dollar-a-day measure for the Millennium Development Goal to halve world poverty. It is an important question, since if the human poverty index had been chosen instead, the Millennium Development Goal would not have been met. The key lesson of the class is that methodological choices matter—a theme that runs through the course.

In the 'culture' module, students examine the contributions and limitations of ethnography as a research method and then use an ethnographic study of Madagascar to explore the impact of attitudes and beliefs on the effectiveness of a World Bank conservation strategy. This highlights how introducing new types of evidence can broaden the scope of analysis and lead to different conclusions, while also demonstrating the role of different kinds of explanation.[2] Later in the term, students analyse declassified primary source documents from the Kremlin and Central Intelligence Agency and assess the role of agency, structure and ideas in explaining the end of the Cold War. In this they are contrasting the formal methods of international relations, and their emphasis on generalization, with the different types of questions and the primary-source-based methodologies of historians, which highlight the specificities of particular historical events.

In the module on the financial crisis, students explore causal explanations, first by considering the interpretation and limitations of graphical evidence on individual contributory factors, then by considering evidence for and against Raghuram Rajan's argument that growing inequality was

---

[2]While our economic models provide powerful insights into how extrinsic factors influence the actions of economic agents, ethnographies, for example, provide complementary insights into the meanings people attach to their actions and thereby enhance students' awareness of economic actors as reflexive agents. In this way, exposure to alternative methodologies serves to enhance economics students' understanding of both the value of economic models and of their limitations.

a cause of the crisis (Rajan 2010), and, finally, by exploring the complex combination of factors contributing to the European debt crisis as part of a formal, if stylized, exercise in conjunctural causation.

Skill development is embedded not only in classes, but also in the lectures. A series of six 'special lectures', one per module, provides a more in-depth treatment of issues such as causality in the social sciences (as part of the financial crisis module), argumentation and the role of questions in research and learning. In addition, LSE100 has used instant voting systems ('clickers') to facilitate active learning in lectures, enabling a degree of participation and two-way communication even in very large lectures.

LSE100 has been designed for students from across the social sciences and, in helping all students to develop an awareness of alternative disciplinary approaches, yields common benefits to all of them, regardless of their 'home' department. At the same time, the impact and role of the course is different for each discipline.

The multidisciplinary approach aims, in the first instance, to foster economics students' development of that 'combination of gifts' described by Keynes as essential to economic understanding. In other words, introducing students to different disciplinary approaches—especially when applied to the same problem, as in LSE100—is a way to open up their thinking to multiple strands of analysis. No real-world problem fits neatly into an 'economics' box: there are elements that can only be fully understood by drawing on the insights and analytical tools of other disciplines. Enabling students to explore new disciplinary approaches and to confront different ways of approaching the same problem can enhance their ability to think creatively about new problems. At the same time, the exposure to alternative disciplinary perspectives can help them to develop a critical understanding of economics.

It can also deepen their understanding of the role and interpretation of models. In introducing second-year microeconomic theory, my colleague Margaret Bray discusses the role of models using the example of the map of the London Underground. The well-known Tube map is a simplified, schematic representation that was designed to help Tube travellers. If you are navigating London by Tube, the Tube map is clear and easy to use. It is a great map ('model')—*for that purpose*. But if you try to use the Tube map to navigate London by foot, you may get hopelessly lost, since positions on the Tube map may bear little relation to true geographic positions. The Tube map was designed for the particular purpose of enabling individuals to get around London by Tube. In the same way, economic models are simplified and stylized representations of particular economic relationships or transactions or institutions, designed to highlight certain relevant features with the aim of understanding those features and their implications more clearly. Introducing students to a variety of different models or theories outside of economics can help them to clarify the role of abstraction in advancing our understanding and to appreciate how theoretical models are inevitably selective. Indeed, it teaches them that they are selective by design: that is what makes them theories.

Introducing students to a variety of models drawn from different disciplines can also enhance their understanding of causal explanations. While the introduction to multiple regression takes economics students beyond simple monocausal explanations, they may still confuse correlation with causation. An overemphasis on a narrow range of models may obscure the complexity of economic relationships and transactions, making students less aware of possible confounding influences and the risk of spurious correlation. Causality may be seen simply as a temporal relation by economics students, a notion often given misleading legitimacy through applications of 'Granger causality' tests (see Helm (1984, p. 124) and LeRoy (2004) for a discussion of these issues). Exposure to different disciplinary perspectives can foster an awareness of more complex causal explanations that may, for example, involve combinations of necessary and sufficient causes.

Put another way, the combination of an introduction to alternative disciplinary approaches and a greater emphasis on inductive approaches can increase students' awareness, as they progress in their studies, of what lies behind the common assumption in economics of *ceteris paribus*. It can help students to understand the nature of the valid causal claims we are able to make as economists and to understand how the complexity of economic interactions limits us, as Hicks emphasized, to weak explanations about the effect of a change in a particular variable *all things being equal* (Helm 1984). Engaging with causal explanations can help students to understand how almost any empirical test in economics is a test of a large number of joint hypotheses, including a related set of theoretical concepts as well as of empirical definitions and measures.[3]

Introducing a multidisciplinary element can also deepen our students' understanding of economics in other important ways. For example, it

---

[3]See Helm (1984) for an insightful assessment of Hicks's arguments and the related Quine–Duhem thesis. Helm cites the example of Friedman's permanent income hypothesis as an illustration of how economic claims involve a complex 'network of theories and beliefs' and a 'nest of supporting hypotheses'.

can foster a greater appreciation of the broader institutional, cultural and historical context for economic analysis and an awareness of how economic behaviour and institutions may consequently change over time.

The approach adopted in LSE100 has its challenges. First among these is designing a curriculum that is accessible and engaging for such a heterogeneous cohort of students, coming from different departments and degree programmes. Another is providing the substantial support and training necessary to enable the class teachers to teach confidently outside of their discipline. Yet another challenge is developing the systems and resources necessary, with a cohort of 1,250 students, to provide the high level of feedback needed to support self-reflection and skill development.

But the approach has also yielded some side-benefits. It provides students with the opportunity to engage in current issues of public debate, which might not otherwise happen in their degree programme, it brings them into contact with leading researchers from across the LSE, and it helps to create a stronger common intellectual experience for undergraduates at the LSE.

By providing students with an opportunity to confront different disciplinary approaches in thinking about important current issues, LSE100 aims to help them to become more independent and critical thinkers, with a better understanding of deductive and inductive approaches and the skills and breadth of thinking they need to apply economics more effectively to real-world problems.

REFERENCES

Eichengreen, B. 2009. The last temptation of risk. *The National Interest*, May/June issue. Available at http://nationalinterest.org/article/the-last-temptation-of-risk-3091.

Friedman, M. 1953. *Essays in Positive Economics.* University of Chicago Press.

Helm, D. 1984. Predictions and causes: a comparison of Friedman and Hicks on method. *Oxford Economic Papers (New Series)* 36 (Supplement: Economic Theory and Hicksian Themes):118–134 (www.jstor.org/stable/2662840).

LeRoy, S. 2004. Causality in economics. Technical Report 20/04, Centre for Philosophy of Natural and Social Sciences, London School of Economics.

Rajan, R. 2010. *Fault Lines: How Hidden Fractures Still Threaten the World Economy.* Princeton University Press.

CHAPTER TWENTY-TWO

What Do Students Need?

By Alison Wride

For those of us teaching in UK universities, the decade leading up to the crisis presented a number of challenges: low inflation, falling unemployment, stable (if slightly underwhelming), the introduction of an apparently successful single currency across much of Europe. Of course all of these might be viewed as unequivocal 'good things', but in terms of attracting students to study economics and keeping their interest when they were with us, the macroeconomics of the decade lacked drama and issues. And it is probably true that the decade had a similar impact on those of us standing at the front of the lecture theatre. It is unlikely that many academics really believed that boom and bust was dead, but equally it is hardly surprising if a certain amount of complacency creeps in when updating last year's teaching materials just calls for one extra line of data on your slides. It was not all bad news, of course, particularly for microeconomics. As macroeconomics appeared more straightforward, we were able to carve out more time to spend with students on the problems and issues that excited their interest. We looked closely at all aspects of market failure, discussed green issues in depth and introduced increasingly sophisticated aspects of behavioural economics, even into beginner-level teaching. That last sentence has a hollow tone and you would have to be pretty thick skinned not to flinch at our complacency now, and not to spend at least a little time contemplating how culpable we were.

So where does this leave economists now? With our reputations in tatters, hanging our heads and shuffling our feet in shame? Or with an unrivalled opportunity to shake up what we have taught and how we have taught it? It may be a combination of the two, but we will lose all credibility if we come out of the crisis without learning from it and changing what we do. We currently see unprecedented interest in the discipline and a sense of urgency that has been missing for years. Since 2008 the number of applicants to university courses involving economics has risen substantially: disproportionately compared with other subjects. We could posit a number of drivers for this increase: the economic downturn encouraging applicants towards subjects that are more vocational, a greater interest in economics given the crisis, or even an increased aware-ness of economics from those who had not previously appreciated what it involved. No matter what the reason, it presents us with the opportu-nity to better educate this generation and to develop greater robustness for the discipline, from both academic economists and practitioners.

Before thinking about what students need, it is worth spending some time mulling over what they want. There is a case to argue that stu-dents now are not so very different from those of previous years: they want to enjoy university, find their degree interesting and get a good job after graduating. But while those three principles hold true, the focus has moved markedly towards careers and employability. The single most common question I have been asked at open days since the introduction of variable fees is: 'What can I do afterwards?' During their time at univer-sity many students are ruthlessly focused on getting a job, sometimes to the exclusion of developing an in-depth appreciation of the subject they are studying. If that sounds critical, it certainly is not meant to be. With students graduating in 2012 having a typical total student loan debt of £20,000, and with that figure projected to rise to £40,000 by 2015, it is entirely rational for students to prioritize employability skills over aca-demic content.

How have universities and, more pertinently, economics departments responded to this changing agenda? The answer varies considerably across the higher education sector. Many of the newer universities have been proactively honing their students' transferable skills for years, while the more traditional have relied on the quality of their intake and the aca-demic content of their degrees. More recently, the latter have changed their approach, with an intense focus on graduate employability, work experience and graduate salaries. However, it would be true to say that academic economists have not always wholeheartedly engaged with this process. 'Group work? Only leads to free-riding. Presentation skills? You can't do that for mathematical topics. Employability? There will always be jobs for our students. Essays and report writing? That's fine for business studies.' Of course, not all economists take this approach and we do see many of our students getting good jobs, but I do wonder if sometimes that has been despite, rather than because of, the attitude of some within the discipline.

So if students *want* great careers, whether as economists or otherwise, what do they *need*? Many economists believe the answer lies in more mod-els and better models. Yet the curriculum for single honours economics is stuffed with models and, in most cases, it has become increasingly technical over the last twenty years. Some may find that surprising, given the general acceptance that the mathematical background of university entrants is weaker than it was in the past. However, if we think about what drives the content of modules and lectures, we can see why it has happened. Most academics undertake both research and teaching, and they are most comfortable when their teaching and research interests coincide. If you also appreciate that the most valued research outputs in economics tend to be the most technical, then you will see how we have reached this position. It may not be helpful to ascribe blame, but there is little doubt that successive Research Assessment Exercises have ramped up the value put on technical research and consequently have had unintended (but unsurprising) consequences for the teaching of economics.

Does this matter? After all, economics is a technical subject and it does involve both mathematics and statistics, so how can it possibly be detrimental if students are taught in a technical way and we have models galore? The answer is that it does matter, because of what we have lost. The concentration on the most mathematical areas to the exclusion of others has resulted in a generation of graduates many of whom find it difficult to apply simple principles to economic problems. The technical models have driven out 'thinking like an economist'. Some evidence to back up this proposition lies within the annual recruitment process of the Government Economic Service. In many cases, the service finds that applicants cannot apply even basic theory to simple case studies: they have little understanding of the power that lies in the microeconomic tools that they have acquired. This in itself is cause for concern, but perhaps even more disappointing is the growing realization that many of those students do not even really fully acquire the technical skills; instead, they know just enough to get through the assessments. Contributory factors include fewer small classes, larger numbers of modules, increased reliance on multiple choice questions and online assessment, and students who, after years of SATs, GCSEs, AS and A levels have become exceptionally good at taking exams.

Earlier in this chapter I referred to our culpability; but if you asked me to what extent universities are to blame, I am not sure I could answer. Did the crisis emerge because we did not teach people properly, or because we taught them too well? If our mistake was inappropriate regulation, then perhaps we should look at the teaching of economics in the seventies and eighties rather than over the last decade. If we think that poor information was the key, then it may be true that the neoclassical model remains the appropriate basis for undergraduate teaching. Even as we talked about behavioural economics and patted ourselves on the backs for understanding how well people respond to incentives, we did little to press governments on what this might mean for our laws and our systems. The teaching of economics has been premised on the basis that it should be value-free; if we persist with this, are we happy to accept the consequences? Perhaps the time has come to see normative economics as something that should no longer be treated as a bolt-on extra to 'proper economics', to positive theories and principles. I do know that we have sent out graduates, many of whom have gone on to important roles in industry and the country, who have consistently undervalued risk and have not seen 'right and wrong' as anything to do with economics.

So what changes does the discipline need? Can we send out economists with both great technical skills and the ability to think? I think the answer is that, while we need both, lack of the latter is what will bring us down. So, rather than assuming that what we research must be what students need, we should talk to government and to industry to find out what skills they want graduates to have. If we do that and if we also revisit what studying for a degree means, if we can allow students to challenge us, if we can reward enquiring minds rather than model answers, if we are prepared to say that sometimes we do not know the answer and that students should think things through themselves, then perhaps we can give them both what they want and what they need.

Acknowledgements

This book has its origins in a conference on 7 February 2012, organized by the Government Economic Service (GES) and hosted by the Bank of England. I am extremely grateful to Andy Ross, Deputy Director of the GES, and Andrew Haldane of the Bank of England for their enthusiastic interest in the issues discussed in this book, and for supporting the conference and its follow-up. Warmest thanks also to all their colleagues involved in the organization. In addition to all the contributors to this volume, I would also like to thank Mark Beatson of FTI Consulting, Adam Cellan-Jones, Professor Nick Crafts of Warwick University, Professor Jonathan Haskel of Imperial College Business School, Geoff Riley and Jim Riley of tutor2u, Paolo Siciliani, Professor Peter Sinclair of Birmingham University and Romesh Vatilingam.

Diane Coyle, September 2012

About Enlightenment Economics

Enlightenment Economics, which has supported the publication of this book, is a London-based consultancy specializing in the economic and social effects of new technologies, with expertise on technology markets, innovation and competition policy, corporate governance and globalization. Recent projects have included assessment of the impact of mobile telephony in developing economies, research on the use of new technologies and social networking in disasters, work on innovation systems, and on the social impacts of information and communication technologies.

See www.enlightenmenteconomics.com for more information.

About London Publishing Partnership

The London Publishing Partnership is a publishing services company that specializes in working with researchers, learned societies, research institutes, think-tanks and also individual authors. We can provide the following services.

- Consultancy on editorial, production and marketing strategies for books at the individual-title and whole-programme levels.
- High-quality and speedy production work (copy-editing, typesetting, proofreading, artwork, indexing, project management).
- Management of the printing, order fulfilment and distribution of books, or the production and distribution of eBooks and downloads.
- Tailor-made marketing and publicity campaigns (either for individual publications or for an entire programme).

Our emphasis in all that we do is on quality and efficiency. We specialize in working with first-rate academic and professional research organizations and we fully understand their concerns. The company was founded in 2010 and our institutional client list includes the Centre for Economic Performance, the Paul Woolley Centre for the Study of Capital Market Dysfunctionality, the International Growth Centre, and the Centre for Economic Policy Research. Books for these institutions have been published by us, but under the imprints of our clients. Under our own London Publishing Partnership imprint we have published for Neil Monnery (*Safe as Houses? A Historical Analysis of Property Prices*), Peter Westin (*In From the Cold: The Rise of Russian Capitalism*) and Diane Coyle (*What's the Use of Economics: Teaching the Dismal Science After the Crisis*).

See www.londonpublishingpartnership.co.uk for more information.